Holocene Depositional History and Anasazi Occupation in McElmo Canyon

Arizona State Museum Archaeological Series 188

Holocene Depositional History and Anasazi Occupation in McElmo Canyon, Southwestern Colorado

Eric R. Force and Wayne K. Howell

Arizona State Museum
The University of Arizona®

Arizona State Museum Archaeological Series 188

Arizona State Museum
The University of Arizona
Tucson, Arizona 85721-0026
© 1997 by The Arizona Board of Regents
All rights reserved. Published 1997
Printed in the United States of America

ISBN (paper): 1-889747-53-X

Library of Congress Catalog Card Number: 97-071747

ARIZONA STATE MUSEUM ARCHAEOLOGICAL SERIES

General Editor: E. Charles Adams
Technical Editor: Joanne M. Newcomb

The Archaeological Series of the Arizona State Museum, The University of Arizona, publishes the results of research in archaeology and related disciplines conducted in the Greater Southwest. Original, monograph-length manuscripts are considered for publication, provided they deal with appropriate subject matter. Information regarding procedures or manuscript submission and review may be obtained from the General Editor, Archaeological Series, Arizona State Museum, P.O. Box 210026, The University of Arizona, Tucson, Arizona, 85721-0026; Email: homolovi@ccit.arizona.edu.

Distributed by The University of Arizona Press, 1230 N. Park Avenue, Suite 102, Tucson, Arizona 85719

Contents

List of Figures   vi
Abstract   vii
Responsibility and Acknowledgments   viii

1 The Study   1
    Context   1
        Geologic and Geomorphic Context   1
        Archaeological Context   3
        Analogous Studies   4
    Methods of Study   6
        Geologic Methods   6
        Archaeological Methods   6

2 Fluvial and Archaeological Stratigraphy   11
    Fluvial Deposits   12
        Channel and Floodplain Deposits   12
        Alluvial Fan Deposits   13
        Soils   14
    Archaeological Remains in Stratigraphic Context   14
        Sites Buried in Alluvium   16
        Surface Sites   22
    General Geologic Relations   23
        Morpho-chronologic Relations   23
        Stratigraphic Relations   23
        Areal Relations   24
        Depositional Packages   25
    Summary   28

3 Area History   29
    Geomorphic History   29
    Habitation History   30
        Basketmaker III   30
        Pueblo I   31
        Pueblo II   31
        Pueblo III   32

4 Geomorphic Model and Archaeological Implications   33
    A Depositional-Geomorphic Model   33
    Relations Among Habitation, Environment, and Depositional Regime   35
        Adaptation of Habitation to the Depositional Regime   35
        Relation of Entrenchment to Habitation   36
        The Floodlands as a Habitation Environment   36

References Cited   39

Figures

1.1   Location of the study area relative to some regional geographic and archaeological features   2

1.2   Geologic map of Quaternary units in the McElmo Canyon study area   map envelope

1.3   Terminologies of Anasazi chronology   4

1.4   Alluvial chronologies for the late Holocene   5

1.5   Longitudinal east-west profile of measured sections in alluvium of Anasazi age   7

1.6   Ceramic assemblages recovered from alluvial profiles and habitation sites in the study area   8

2.1   Annotated photo of collapsed structural feature (probably a checkdam) at Kelly Place   11

2.2   Cross-sectional diagram looking east of sedimentary facies at profile 37   12

2.3   Photo of bedding in micaceous sand facies overlying transported ceramics and building stones in profile 2   13

2.4   Annotated photo of cross-section of Anasazi checkdam and resulting paleorelief on surface of northside fan   14

2.5   Fence diagram of depositional facies relative to cultural features in the Kelly Place area   15

2.6   Field drawing of an unconformity looking WNW between floodplain-fan sequences of approximately Basketmaker III and Pueblo III age near profile 32   17

2.7   Photo of pinnacle of Basketmaker III deposits projecting into mantling Pueblo II deposits   18

2.8   Annotated photo of fan-channel gravels containing reworked midden debris of Pueblo II age   19

2.9   Annotated photo of detail of the unconformity revealed by excavation on east side of pinnacle seen in Figure 2.7   20

2.10a   General view of Sue's Ruin (5MT11735) kiva   21

2.10b   Detail of kiva wall showing contact of flood deposits and older cultural material   21

2.11   Longitudinal diagram of depositional packages relative to the unconformity   26

2.12   Graph of age vs. position of aggradation and entrenchment   27

3.1   Sequential diagrams of the relation of stream morphology to habitation   30

3.2   Diagram of envelope of Anasazi-age deposits showing the relations of valley gradients at different periods   31

4.1   Relation of McElmo Canyon hydraulic conditions to entrenchment thresholds   34

Abstract

McElmo Canyon in southwestern Colorado, which drains the Montezuma basin into the San Juan River, contains excellent exposures of Holocene sequences that underlie a broad valley-bottom terrace system. These exposures are the vehicle for this study of the stratigraphy and geometry of fluvial deposits and their contained archaeological remains. Anasazi sites in alluvium range from Basketmaker III to Pueblo III in age, thus providing age guides for the period A.D. 500–1300.

Fluvial deposits include channel, floodplain, and tributary alluvial fan facies. During times when (and at locales where) the system aggraded, these facies are interbedded and gradational in a way that suggests a braided channel, in contrast to degrading episodes that suggest a meandering channel. Local deposition rate was as great as about three meters in 100 years where distal fan deposits on the northern side of the valley are interbedded with main-channel floodplain deposits.

Two main depositional packages are present, separated by an unconformity that mostly formed during the Pueblo I period. The age of this high relief unconformity is apparently diachronous, and the overlying package is certainly diachronous, both suggesting upstream migration of about five kilometers in 200 years.

Our stratigraphic record of migrating loci of entrenchment and aggradation corresponds to studies of modern drainages, in which such changes are internal drainage adjustments. However, the broader time intervals of dominant erosion versus deposition are similar to alluvial chronologies elsewhere in the region and are thought to be controlled by climate change.

An intricate feedback system apparently operated between sedimentary and geomorphic events on one hand, and Anasazi agriculture and habitation on the other. Agricultural water-control features show the importance of actively aggrading toes of northside fans in Anasazi agriculture. Habitation, situated on adjacent quasi-stable landforms, closely tracked loci of aggradation as these loci migrated. No habitation adjacent to valley segments suffering coeval entrenchment was found.

The relation of migrating entrenchment loci and observed Anasazi habitation patterns suggest that the deleterious effects of entrenchment on Anasazi floodland agriculture probably resulted only in migration to nearby loci of deposition. The floodland component of Anasazi agriculture in this region may explain some Anasazi migration patterns that are otherwise anomalous. Adjacent floodlands and uplands, both in zones favorable for agriculture, may be required for successful habitation at certain times. The locations of the zones favorable for each agricultural strategy may vary through time somewhat independently of one another.

Responsibility and Acknowledgments.

This study was conducted in cooperation with the Crow Canyon Archaeological Center (CCAC) and the U.S. Geological Survey. Force is responsible for geologic information. He was aided in the field by his wife Jane. Howell is responsible for archaeological information, with support from Angela Schwab, Bruce Bradley, and Mark Varien of CCAC. Special thanks are due Bill Lipe for helping to organize this project, and Karen Adams, Mark Hovezak, Ruth Slickman, Ricky Lightfoot, and the rest of the CCAC staff for logistical support. The support of Kelly Place is also appreciated; special thanks go to Laura Livingston, Barry Hibbets, and Kristie and Rodney Carriker. For advice on hydrologic aspects of the study we thank Bob Webb, Bill Langer, and Rich Hereford. Reviews by Bob Webb, Carla van West, Richard Hereford, and Jeff Dean improved the manuscript.

Chapter One

The Study

Context

This study examines the relation of sedimentary-geomorphic evolution in a fluvial system to changing human habitation, using their mutual stratigraphy. The research, in the upper Holocene deposits of McElmo Canyon, is the result of informal cooperation between the Crow Canyon Archaeological Center (CCAC) and the U.S. Geological Survey. A geological objective is to use the archaeological remains in the fluvial deposits to provide a chronologic framework for sedimentary features and events recorded in the stratigraphy. An archaeological objective is to use the stratigraphic framework of cultural remains to interpret habitation history. An overall goal is the reconstruction of changing late Holocene environments.

The McElmo drainage has its headwaters in the broad Montezuma Valley to the east, and empties into the San Juan River to the west in Utah (Figure 1.1). The area chosen for study is a central reach of McElmo Canyon that is 7.5 km long, approximately from the junction of Goodman, Trail, and McElmo canyons on the east, to Battle Rock on the west (Figure 1.1). It corresponds to the southern boundary of the Sand Canyon study area of CCAC researchers (Lipe 1992).

McElmo Canyon has several advantages for studies of Holocene fluvial stratigraphy: 1) McElmo Canyon is at the geographic heart of the Mesa Verde region of the Anasazi cultural tradition, and the resulting density of cultural sites (Figure 1.1), many buried in alluvium, makes possible the dating of indi-

vidual sedimentary units and events for the period A.D. 500 to 1300; 2) Post-1880 entrenchment of the valley, due in part to its use as an irrigation flume, has provided superb exposures through as much as 8 meters of alluvium, including that of Anasazi age; 3) The distinctive character and local distribution of source rocks permits determination of source areas for Holocene units. The study area was situated to take optimum advantage of these provenance contrasts.

Geologic and Geomorphic Context

McElmo Canyon is carved into Mesozoic rocks from the Navajo Sandstone through the Dakota Sandstone, which are gently warped to form the south-plunging parts of the McElmo Dome (Ekren and Houser 1965). Tertiary igneous rocks have intruded the sequence south of the canyon.

The outcrop pattern has produced a central reach of McElmo Canyon in which rocks on the north side are reddish sandstones (Lower Jurassic Navajo Sandstone, Middle Jurassic Entrada Sandstone, Middle Jurassic Summerville Formation, and Upper Jurassic Junction Creek Sandstone), overlain by green mudstone and pale sandstone (Upper Jurassic Morrison Formation and mid-Cretaceous Dakota Sandstone). Fine sandstones predominate in this sequence. On the south side, the reddish sequence is more restricted because of the southward plunge of the dome. Therefore, tributaries entering from the north carry pink fine sand and occasionally provide a green mudflow,

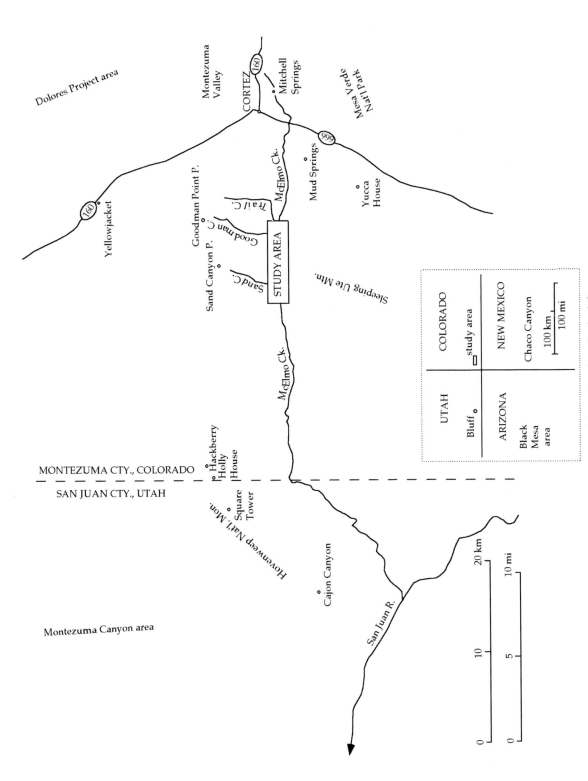

Figure 1.1 Location of the study area relative to some regional geographic and archaeological features.

whereas those entering from the south carry copious clasts of igneous porphyry and brownish sand except in one short interval. The headwaters of McElmo Creek drain large areas of Mancos Shale (Upper Cretaceous), so floodplain deposits tend toward a brown or gray color and contain pebbles that reflect mixed sources. All the Holocene fluvial deposits show these color-coded indications of their derivation.

Plateaus north of the study area are mantled by Pleistocene eolian deposits consisting of silty very fine sand (Price et al. 1988). This loess-like material is pinkish, adding to the source-area effect described above, but is generally absent south of McElmo Canyon. At times when mesa-top soil erosion exceeded slope erosion, sediment supply in the study area was dominated by Pleistocene eolian material.

McElmo Canyon conducts runoff from the highlands around the Montezuma Valley, with elevations of 2100 m (7000 ft) to over 2700 m (9000 ft) (north face of Mesa Verde, northeast slope of Sleeping Ute Mountain), through the Cortez, Colorado area, westward to the San Juan River at an elevation of about 1400 m (4600 ft) (Figure 1.1). The drainage area of the basin is about 875 square kilometers (342 square miles), and the average annual runoff is 1,230 cubic meters (33,250 acre-feet).

The walls of McElmo Canyon are up to 460 m (1500 ft) high on the north side and higher on the south; average slopes are on the order of 10 degrees, though some units form cliffs. Bedrock commonly forms a bank of McElmo Creek, but not the full width of the channel or the valley. Thus the stream bed is free to migrate either horizontally or vertically without eroding bedrock in the study area. Upstream and downstream from the study area, however, the stream bed is locally fixed by bedrock. At the time scale of this study, such points on the stream gradient are probably invariant.

McElmo Creek meanders across a modern floodplain of variable width. These meanders have locally been locked into place by entrenchment (Figure 1.2 in map envelope). Upstream (east) from the study area, entrenched meanders are even more pronounced. The gradient of the creek in the study area is about 7.3 m/km or 0.0073.

Regional geomorphology suggests an extensive history of stream capture in the Quaternary. The McElmo drainage may have pirated its Montezuma Valley headwaters from the southward-flowing Navajo Wash drainage (Wanek 1959). The setting of the Mud Springs archaeological site shows that any such piracy preceded Anasazi occupation. However, the subsequent geomorphologic history may reflect an approach to a new equilibrium. Surficial deposits and geomorphology of McElmo Canyon were not a major focus of Ekren and Houser (1965), and the subject has apparently not been addressed by others.

Archaeological Context

The Anasazi occupied the Four Corners region from before the Christian period to about A.D. 1300. The study area is in the heart of the Mesa Verde Region of Anasazi remains (Figure 1.1). Archaeological research has been conducted in this region for over a century (see Eddy et al. 1984).

The standard Pecos subdivisions of the Anasazi time period (Kidder 1927), along with variations of the standard scheme that are more pertinent to the study region, are shown in Figure 1.3. Each period is characterized by different styles of architecture and pottery, and sub-periods generally can be identified.

Anasazi occupation in the McElmo drainage spans the Basketmaker III–Pueblo III periods, with the mesa tops north of the canyon the favored areas of occupation for all these time periods. Within McElmo Canyon proper, small populations are estimated for the Basketmaker III–Pueblo II periods, with great-

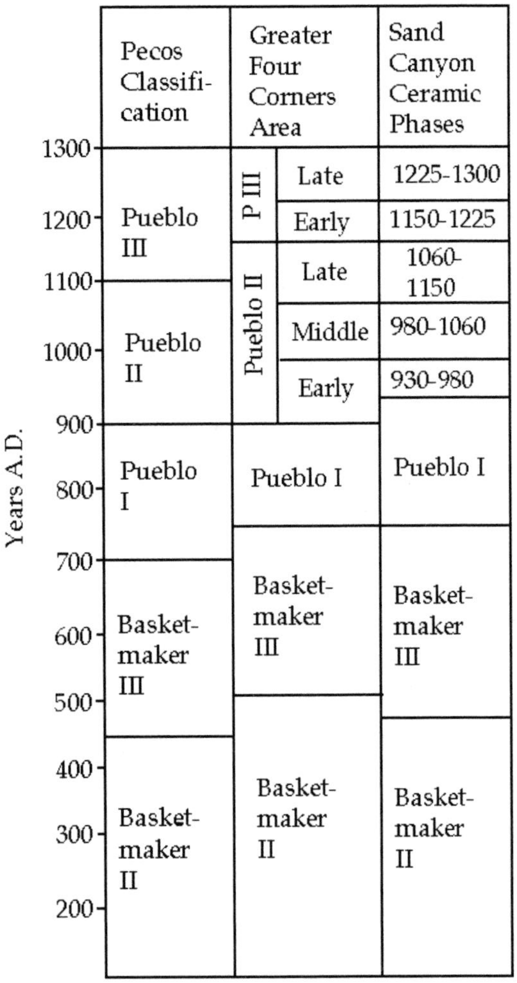

Years A.D.	Pecos Classification	Greater Four Corners Area		Sand Canyon Ceramic Phases
1300		P III	Late	1225-1300
1200	Pueblo III		Early	1150-1225
1100		Pueblo II	Late	1060-1150
1000	Pueblo II		Middle	980-1060
900			Early	930-980
800	Pueblo I	Pueblo I		Pueblo I
700				
600	Basketmaker III	Basketmaker III		Basketmaker III
500				
400				
300	Basketmaker II	Basketmaker II		Basketmaker II
200				

Figure 1.3 Terminologies of Anasazi chronology. The first column presents the traditional Pecos Classification (after Kidder 1927). The second column presents a revision currently used throughout the Four Corners area. The third column is that used in the local area by Crow Canyon Archaeological Center (Adler 1992).

est occupation during the Pueblo III period from A.D. 1150–1300 (Adler 1992; Adler and Metcalf 1991; Gleichman and Gleichman 1992). Estimates of prehistoric populations within the region (Rohn 1989; Van West and Lipe 1992) show average densities as great as about 90 per square kilometer.

Anasazi occupations are indicated in and near the project area by scattered small settlements, limited activity sites, and late in the sequence, cliff dwellings and a moderate-sized village, Castle Rock Pueblo (Figure 1.2). Architectural remains from the Pueblo II and Pueblo III periods are generally most apparent. Prominent sites near the project area include Sand Canyon Pueblo, Goodman Point, Mud Springs, Mitchell Springs, Yucca House, and other ruins (Figure 1.1).

Analogous Studies

The Holocene fluvial geomorphology of the southwestern United States and its relation to the archaeological record is the subject of a rather modest descriptive literature, but a large and contentious literature dealing with process and interpretation. Our citation will not be exhaustive, but concentrates on the most pertinent studies of the late Holocene in the Four Corners region presented to give the reader some concept of the scope of study. Most of the Holocene studies address three main issues: 1) the relative influence of climatic versus purely hydrologic change in controlling deposition and erosion, 2) the direction and type of response to climatic change, and 3) comparisons of prehistoric to historic entrenchment episodes. Few of the studies use a three-dimensional facies approach to Holocene deposition.

In the Black Mesa-Tsegi Canyon area of northeastern Arizona (Figure 1.1), studies of Holocene stratigraphy and geomorphology gave rise to a regional chronostratigraphy (Figure 1.4), based on archaeological, C-14, dendrochronological, and soil-correlation methods in valley cross-sections (Hack 1942; Karlstrom 1988). Correlative environmental studies by Dean (1988) and Hevly (1988) were based on tree-ring and pollen studies, respectively.

In the Chaco Canyon area of northwestern New Mexico (Figure 1.1), studies by Bryan (1954), Hall (1977), and Love (1983a) based on archaeological and C-14 methods, suggest a chronostratigraphic framework somewhat

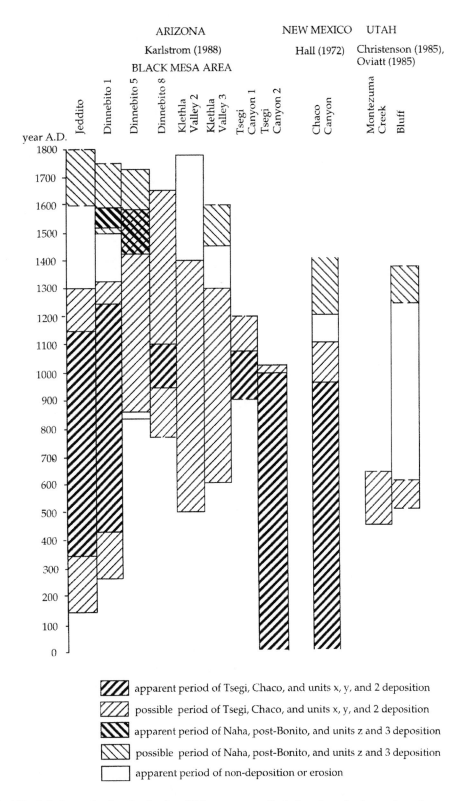

Figure 1.4 Alluvial chronologies for the late Holocene compiled elsewhere in the region. Ages are according to the authors cited; only sections containing Anasazi remains are plotted. Intraformational soils are not plotted due to age uncertainties. Columns with dashed boundaries are approximate; with no boundaries are uncertain. Overlaps are cross-hatched.

similar to that of northern Arizona (Figure 1.4). Love (1979, 1983b) also conducted studies of sedimentary facies and flooding history. Hall (1977) and Betancourt et al. (1983) provide palynologic and packrat-midden information on environmental change, respectively.

In southeastern Utah, Holocene alluvium has been described by Huff and Lesure (1965), Christenson (1985), and Oviatt (1985) in and near Montezuma Canyon (Figure 1.1). Chrono–stratigraphic relations to sequences of Arizona and New Mexico are unclear (Figure 1.4).

In southwestern Colorado, few studies specifically of Holocene fluvial sequences have been conducted. Gillespie (1974) contains a brief, unpublished description of Holocene alluvium in archaeological context near Mesa Verde (Figure 1.1).

Studies of regional environmental change during the period of Anasazi occupation are by Petersen (1988) and D'Arrigo and Jacoby (1991), in addition to studies listed above. Figure 1.3 incorporates Petersen's environmental conclusions for the Dolores archaeological program north of the study area (Figure 1.1). Regional environmental syntheses that incorporate archaeological data include Euler et al. (1979), Dean et al. (1985), Plog et al. (1988), Schlanger (1988), Petersen (1988), Orcutt (1991), and Van West and Lipe (1992).

Methods of Study

This study used methods standard to stratigraphy and archaeology. Where possible we took advantage of feedbacks in which the depositional environment controlled Anasazi land use, which in turn reveals depositional features that otherwise could not be deciphered.

Geologic Methods

Deposits forming the Anasazi terrace were studied by measuring stratigraphic sections of Holocene alluvium where archaeological remains were found to provide age information and/or where excellent exposure provided information on depositional facies. Where possible, the geometry of each sedimentary unit or facies was established. These units were then traced in stratigraphic context and mapped (Figure 1.2).

Measurement of stratigraphic profiles was by steel tape, and vertical control by transit survey. For each interval, sediment character and probable depositional environment were recorded. Special attention was given to: 1) buried soils and unconformities, 2) sediment source, 3) paleocurrent directions, 4) vertical relief on depositional packages, and 5) cultural features diagnostic of environment and/or age. Thirteen profiles were measured bed-by-bed, and eleven more with more generalized methods.

The geologic map (Figure 1.2) subdivides Quaternary deposits by age and depositional environment. The map shows the deposit type dominating the first meter below the ground surface, rather than the section as a whole. This map also shows as numbered points the measured stratigraphic profiles.

These two types of information are combined as an east-west longitudinal section along the valley (Figure 1.5), showing the vertical relationship of the deposits of Holocene age. Deposits unique to the north but not the south side of the valley are included, so that the section can be considered a section along the northern margin of the valley. Each section shows sediment facies and the age of buried cultural features.

Archaeological Methods

Archaeological work focused on providing a chronologic framework and the general interpretation of habitation environment. Data were gathered by surface reconnaissance, and from previous informal excavations. Most archaeo-

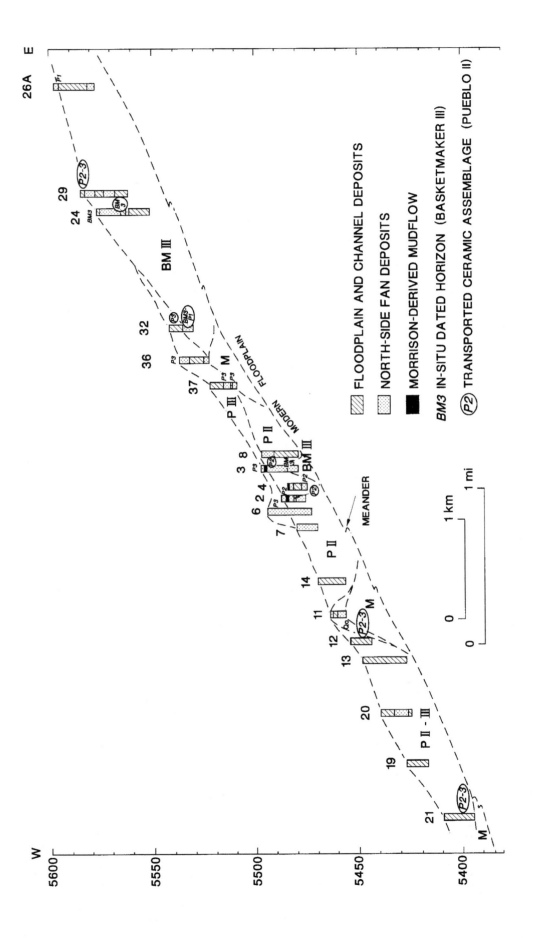

Figure 1.5 Longitudinal east-west profile of measured sections in alluvium of Anasazi age, positioned with topographic data and transit surveys, showing sediment facies and age of buried cultural features along north side of valley. Gradient of modern drainage (from topographic contours only) is also shown. Unit designations as for Figure 1.2, except units of Anasazi age subdivided as much as possible.

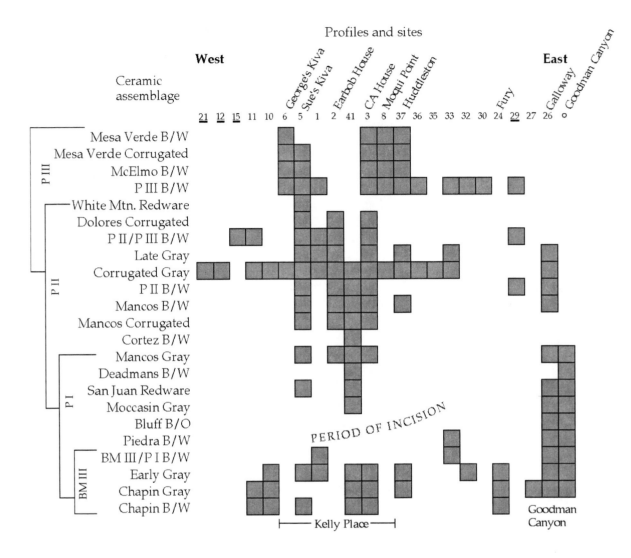

Figure 1.6 Ceramic assemblages recovered from alluvial profiles and habitation sites in the study area. Ceramic types arranged from earliest to latest appearance, with long-lived types adjusted to reflect assemblages, and presented on an east-west longitudinal axis through the study area. Types not encountered in the study area are not included in the listing. Underlined numbers are detrital assemblages only.

logical dating for this project relies on ceramic fragments recovered from buried sedimentary horizons and habitation sites (Figure 1.4). Some ceramic samples were analyzed by CCAC laboratory personnel, and others were identified in the field. Larger buried remains were also used to date enclosing sediments; these included originally above-ground masonry room blocks, subterranean kivas, pit houses, and refuse middens. Each such feature is typically associated with ceramic fragments. In addition, four

check dams that could only be broadly dated give information on sediment transport relative to Anasazi agriculture. Tree-ring and C-14 data have not been used in this study because of the comparative abundance of other datable material.

The use of ceramics for dating is based on comparison with defined wares, types, and assemblages recovered from tree-ring dated contexts (Figure 1.6). The precision of this cross-dating approach is limited by sample size; small samples may indicate no better than 150–250 year age intervals, whereas larger assemblages can indicate intervals of 50 years or less during certain periods. Even single sherds recovered from buried contexts are commonly useful as horizon markers, particularly for the appearance of gray ware ceramics by A.D. 575, of neck banded types after A.D. 775, and of surface corrugation after A.D. 900. Temporal placement of sites and ceramic assemblages is based on comparison with types and assemblages as described by Blinman (1986), Blinman and Wilson (1989), and Breternitz et al. (1974).

The contexts in which archaeological remains were found vary from bedrock sites with unknown relation to alluvium, through sites on alluvial surfaces, to multicomponent sites buried in alluvium. In addition, profiles and sites containing ceramic fragments vary from in situ assemblages to detrital contexts. The various contexts are treated separately because each has differing age implications.

In situ ceramic assemblages represent occupied land surfaces, and are associated with buried soils or unconformities, middens, hearths, and structures. These in situ assemblages give a true age for the surface between two fluvial deposits, but mixed ages in these assemblages may represent an age span of occupation, reuse of older artifacts, and/or reoccupation of older surfaces.

In contrast, some ceramic fragments are detrital, commonly enclosed in sandy or gravelly sediment. These ceramics give only a maximum age for the associated deposit. Thus their interpretation is inherently ambiguous.

Two circumstances common in the study area give detrital ceramics more value in chronology. First, in a few places, in situ ceramic fragments in an overlying horizon have provided a minimum age for the detrital assemblage, which coupled with its inherent maximum age, yield an age interval. Second, numerous detrital fragments locally represent the same time period and show little evidence of transport. This could reflect either coeval adjacent habitation, or erosion of an earlier midden or buried soil nearby. In the latter case, the ceramics give a maximum age of the detrital layer, and a true age of the correlative parent feature (for example, profile 24). In such special cases the significance of the detrital assemblage approaches that of an in situ assemblage. Detrital assemblages are shown separately on Figure 1.5.

Multiple horizons with ceramic fragments have been found in some sections, mostly in the same areas where buried structures occur. This permits age division of some sections and determines minimum accumulation rates for others. Through large parts of the study area, however, ceramic fragments have been found in one horizon at best. Such shortage of datable material has required attempts to trace dated horizons from archaeologically productive sites into barren alluvium.

Chapter Two

Fluvial and Archaeological Stratigraphy

A terrace about 6 m to 9 m (20 ft to 30 ft) above stream level commonly extends almost the full width of the valley floor. In other places this terrace is represented only by erosional remnants along the northern side of the valley, dissected by younger terraces and the modern floodplain (Figure 1.2). The late Holocene sediments of Anasazi age that form this terrace are the subject of this study. This terrace system will be referred to generically as the Anasazi terrace; in detail, several terraces are present.

Where the Anasazi terrace abuts steep tributaries of the main drainage, the terrace generally shows an apex formed on relict fans (Figure 1.2). These may be truncated or entrenched by modern tributary streams. In a few tributaries, the relict fan surface extends up the tributary valley as lateral terraces, as in Sand Canyon.

Numerous small, discontinuous alluvial terraces slightly lower than those of Anasazi age are found throughout the length of the study area (Figure 1.2). Some of these terraces are set into scalloped erosional margins of the Anasazi-age terrace. Apparently they are of post-Anasazi but prehistoric age. Such an inset terrace on Kelly Place is separated from deposits of the adjacent Anasazi terrace by a collapsed Anasazi structure, probably a checkdam (Figure 2.1). The shapes of the inset margins (Figure 1.2) strongly suggest that deposits of the younger terraces filled in entrenched meanders cut through the Anasazi terraces, and aerial photos of them show meander scars. These younger terraces have not been studied, but should hold important clues to the chronology of post-Anasazi stream morphology and entrenchment.

Pre-Holocene gravel fans and fan-terraces are extensive on the south side of the valley (Figure 1.2 and Ekren and Houser 1965). They are derived from the Sleeping Ute Mountains to the south, and carry coarse detritus of porphyry. The few older gravel terraces on the north side of the valley seem to be remnants of channel deposits graded to a former bedrock spillway north of Battle Rock (Figure 1.2).

Figure 2.1 Annotated photo of collapsed structural feature (probably a checkdam) along the unconformity separating deposits of the Anasazi terrace to the left from a younger inset terrace to the right, Kelly Place (5MT11741). Annotations: Qp, Pueblo II deposits; Qy, younger deposits.

Fluvial Deposits

The fluvial deposits of Holocene age occur as channel, floodplain, and fan deposit types. Each of these types is present in deposits of different ages, including modern deposits. Channel and floodplain deposits, formed from precursors of the main McElmo Creek, can in turn be divided into two facies, a braided facies most commonly in association with Anasazi remains, and a meandering facies most commonly in younger inset terraces, modern deposits, and apparently in association with an unconformity within deposits of the Anasazi terrace.

Channel and Floodplain Deposits

Braided facies

Main-drainage deposits of channel and floodplain type intergrade in deposits of Basketmaker III to Pueblo III age in the study area. Gravelly sand channel deposits are in thin cross-sets showing nearly unidirectional transport, indicative of deposition in a braided fluvial system. Deposits clearly of floodplain origin are brown to gray muddy sands and sandy muds, laminated to root-mottled, commonly with thin laminae of better-sorted sand. Individual beds are mostly 2 to 10 cm thick and commonly show a thin upward-coarsening interval succeeded upward by a thicker upward-fining interval. Thin incipient paleosols are present in most sections. This floodplain facies characteristically pinches out by lapping onto sloping substrates such as fan deposits on the sides of the valley, sometimes repeatedly in the same section (Figure 2.2). Thin interbeds of pink sand, some upward-fining, reflect distal fan deposits.

Deposits clearly of main-channel origin are lenticular gravels, commonly with cobbles and pebbles showing westward transport by their imbrication. Clast lithologies include igneous porphyry and silicified green Morrison mudstone, indicating sources from both sides of the valley. Sand and thin clay layers are interbedded with individual channel-fill gravels.

Deposits of intermediate character are mostly finely laminated sands with variable mud content, locally with abundant mica and platy organic matter parallel to bedding. Lamination is predominantly planar, but some cross-lamination representing ripples and small dunes

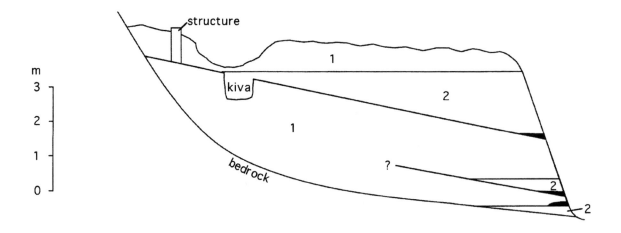

Figure 2.2 Cross-sectional diagram looking east of sedimentary facies at profile 37. Vertical dimension to scale at cut-bank, otherwise schematic. 1, fan deposits; 2, floodplain deposits; shaded, middens of Pueblo III age.

is present and shows westward transport (Figure 2.3). Beds up to about one meter thick are mostly upward-fining. Thin pavements of pebbles are present at the bases of some beds. Where the channel was constricted, this facies may be repeatedly interbedded with fan facies (Figures 1.5 and 2.3).

Meandering Facies
In contrast to the braided facies described above, fluvial deposits of three ages suggest a meandering system: 1) modern deposits of McElmo Creek; 2) small terraces, arcuate in map view, cut into the Anasazi terrace, which show the internal structures of point bars and cut banks, cross-beds with considerable variation in dip direction, and in air photos show meander scars on their upper surfaces; and 3) the unconformity between deposits of Basketmaker III and Pueblo II to III deposits, whose morphology also suggests a meandering system. Distal floodplain lithologies of these deposits are similar to those in the braided facies, but gradations to channel deposits separated by intermediate deposits are lacking.

Alluvial Fan Deposits

Northside Fans
Alluvial fans derived from tributaries entering from the north are volumetrically and areally an important part of the Holocene valley fill, and are especially important in Anasazi occupation and agriculture. These fans are localized around and downstream of the mouths of tributaries on the northern side of the valley (Figure 1.2). Those that are not too deeply dissected or buried still show relict apices in or adjacent to those tributaries.

These fans consist mostly of massive, moderately sorted pinkish sand; very fine sand predominates in many beds. Channel facies of each fan are thick cobble and boulder beds, in which imbricated clasts show southward trans-

Figure 2.3 Photo of bedding in micaceous sand facies overlying transported ceramics and building stones in profile 2. Northside fan deposits underlie field of view.

port. Buried fan surfaces are locally draped by greenish mudflows up to 0.5 m thick, apparently derived from the Morrison Formation, which reveal former fan shapes. Cross-bedding where visible in the sand shows southward and/or radial transport. Steps in depositional surfaces at Anasazi checkdams also show southward transport (Figure 2.4). Fan shape is demonstrably asymmetric in some fans (Figure 1.2), with fan toes "dragged" westward (downstream) and locally interbedded with the intermediate facies of the channel-floodplain assemblage (Figure 2.3).

The massive and sorted nature of the pink sands is partly a reflection of the homogeneity and the similarity of their only apparent sources, i.e., Pleistocene eolian deposits and the sorted sandstones of the Navajo through Dakota Formations. Thus, change in sedimentary process may not have produced much change in supply, and bedding contrast is minimal. Bio-

Figure 2.4 Annotated photo of cross-section of Anasazi checkdam and resulting paleorelief on surface of northside fan, draped by main-channel flood deposits, profile 4 (5MT11742). A ceramic fragment of Pueblo II age was exposed by erosion after the photo was taken. Annotations: 1, fan deposits; 2, floodplain deposits; 3, location of PII ceramic fragment.

turbation has clearly increased homogeneity, and eolian processes may have also.

Southside Fans

Alluvial fans derived from tributaries on the south side of the valley are an important component of valley fill, but some and perhaps all are older than Anasazi occupation (Figure 1.2). These fans are more gravelly than those on the north side, presumably because the porphyry in the southern source is less friable than sandstone in the northern source. In distal portions, these fans are sandy, and such sands may be pink where reddish sandstone is present to the south, as near Ute Creek (Figure 1.2). In such places, derivation from the south is indicated only by relict fan morphology and layers of imbricated porphyry gravel showing northward transport.

Soils

Holocene deposits of the study area commonly contain incipient soils. Frequently, they are associated with charcoal and/or other evidence of habitation. The buried soils (paleosols) are found in both floodplain and fan deposits; the upper surfaces of buried fan deposits commonly show a soil horizon. Greenish mudflow deposits that drape northside fans are a common parent material of these soils.

The buried soils encountered in the study area are less well-developed than those at or near the present surface of the terrace. Commonly the buried soils are marked only by a granular organic layer as much as a few centimeters thick, with little obvious accumulation of clay and carbonate below. Thus, such buried soils belong to stage I carbonate morphology (cf. Birkeland et al. 1991). The thinner and least-distinct soils characterize the more rapidly accumulated sequences.

Archaeological Remains in Stratigraphic Context

Ceramic assemblages provide dates for 37 horizons in 22 of the measured profiles. Five profiles contain only detrital ceramics. In profiles 1, 2, 3, 24, 26, 32, and 37, multiple buried horizons can be dated. The ceramic assemblages are not described individually except in spe-

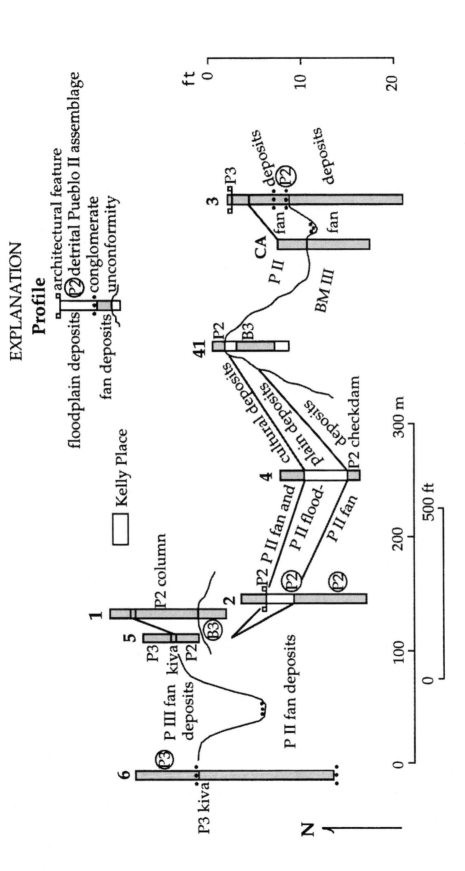

Figure 2.5 Fence diagram of depositional facies relative to cultural features in the Kelly Place area shown on enlarged topographic base. Locations of profiles plotted at top of column. Site notations as in Figure 1.5.

cial cases. They are shown on Figure 1.6, and most are located areally on Figure 1.2 and stratigraphically on Figures 1.5 and 2.5.

Fifteen architectural sites were identified. Ten are habitations containing at least 15 temporal components, and five are limited-use sites or specialized features. All sites were assignable to temporal periods, with varying degrees of precision. Recorded sites are numbered in the Smithsonian trinomial system (5MT prefix). Sites encountered during the course of this project, but not formally recorded, are either designated with the name of the landowner or by a commonly applied place name. All of the habitation sites showed evidence of prior looting and surface collection.

Archaeological sites and ceramic assemblages occur in three depositional contexts: 1) those buried in Anasazi-age floodplains; 2) those buried in northside fans; and 3) those exposed on the surfaces of Anasazi-age alluvial terraces, southside fans, or bedrock. Site descriptions for each depositional context are presented sequentially from upstream (east) to downstream. Sites can be located by reference to associated profiles shown on Figures 1.2, 1.5 and 2.5.

Sites Buried In Alluvium

Floodplain-related Sites

Floodplains of Anasazi age are dated by five buried architectural sites. Most of these sites are only shallowly buried, but correspond in adjacent stratigraphic profiles to buried horizons related to floodplains. Anasazi floodplains are also dated by ceramics in profiles 12, 21, and 24 (Figure 1.6; profiles contain detrital ceramics only). Floodplain deposition apparently occurred in the Basketmaker III, middle and late Pueblo II, and Pueblo III periods.

A shallowly buried stone-lined fire hearth was found at profile 32 (Figure 1.2) upstream of Graveyard Canyon. It was excavated into interbedded fan and floodplain deposits of probable Basketmaker III or Pueblo I age (based on a single detrital sherd), and was buried by floodplain and fan deposits of probable Pueblo III age (also based on a single sherd). The firepit is thus on a significant unconformity that can be traced southward from profile 32 (Figure 2.6) and is described below. Both sequences are better dated at nearby exposures.

Just down-valley, a checkdam at profile 42 is exposed in cross-section in a cut-bank. It consists of three courses of stones and is about 30 cm high. The top of the checkdam coincides with the surface of a small terrace set into a larger, higher, and older terrace. The checkdam is oriented perpendicular to the flow of McElmo Creek, and is surrounded by typical floodplain deposits. Apparently it was situated to retard main-drainage flow along the northern periphery of the floodplain. The checkdam was built on lower floodplain deposits 2.2 m thick overlying bedrock. Probably these sediments postdate the apparent unconformity between these deposits and those of the higher terrace. No ceramics were found. Relations nearby (as at profile 32) suggest that the unconformity was cut on deposits of Basketmaker III age. The checkdam and enclosing deposits are probably Pueblo II to III in age. Water control devices are generally not documented in the Southwest prior to A.D. 900 (Cordell 1984; Rohn 1989), and probably did not become common until A.D. 1100–1150 (Euler 1988; Winter 1977).

The Huddleston site (5MT2883; profile 37) is an early Pueblo III habitation consisting of a small room block, kiva, and midden. The room block is on the terrace surface at the base of a bedrock slope, buried only by thin fan deposits. A kiva is exposed in a small arroyo between the room block and a cutbank to the south, and is buried both by this upper fan and some underlying floodplain deposits. The measured profile in the cutbank exposes both these

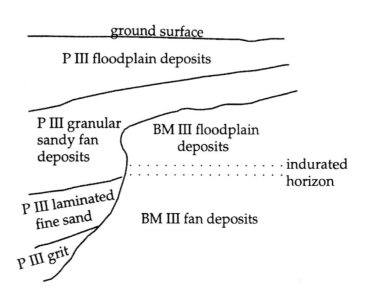

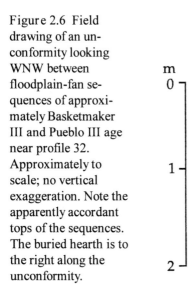

Figure 2.6 Field drawing of an un-conformity looking WNW between floodplain-fan sequences of approximately Basketmaker III and Pueblo III age near profile 32. Approximately to scale; no vertical exaggeration. Note the apparently accordant tops of the sequences. The buried hearth is to the right along the unconformity.

units, but with much thicker (1.9 m) floodplain deposits. A detrital cactus-spine accumulation, probably a reworked and transported packrat midden, lies near the base of the floodplain deposits. These lie in turn on a lower gravelly pink-sand fan deposit, locally mantled by Pueblo III middens. The above-described cultural features were probably built into and on this lower fan deposit (Figure 2.2). Its upper surface is probably erosional, as it slopes more steeply southward than would a depositional surface on a northside fan. Several dark artifact-bearing horizons containing Pueblo III ceramics are present lower in the profile (Figures 1.5 and 2.2) on incipiently weathered surfaces separating floodplain deposits and thin fan deposits as much as 4.7 m below the terrace surface. Correlation of these lower middens with the room block is unclear. The floodplain deposits in this section record a total of about 40 floods during Pueblo III time.

At Kelly Place, site 5MT11742 (profile 4), is a checkdam exposed in a cutbank, 3 m below the surface of the Anasazi terrace. The checkdam appears in cross-section and consists of four courses of unshaped sandstone blocks that stand 70 cm high (Figure 2.4). It was posi-

tioned parallel to the main channel of McElmo Creek to check the flow of water and sediment discharging from a northside tributary, as indicated by south-dipping pink sand almost graded to its upper surface on the north side, but 25 cm below the upper surface on the south side (Figure 2.4). The checkdam is overlain by floodplain deposits that preserve a "snapshot" of sediment transport and the workings of the dam. No paleosol is apparent at this horizon, so the dam was probably situated close to the aggrading stream. The floodplain deposits pinch out to the north as they lap onto the fan (Figure 2.5). A late Pueblo II ceramic fragment (Mancos Black-on-white) was found with the deeply buried checkdam (Figure 2.4), so a post-A.D. 975 date is inferred for this feature. Other buried checkdams in the study area give no stratigraphic information, but one other is oriented to check the flow of water from northside drainages. One at profile 42 is oriented differently (described above), and another (5MT11741) lies slumped on a former cutbank slope along an unconformity at Kelly Place (Figure 2.1).

Earbob House (5MT11740; profile 2) is located on the south edge of the terrace at Kelly

Figure 2.7 Annotated photo of pinnacle of Basketmaker III deposits projecting into mantling Pueblo II deposits such that the tops of the sequences are apparently accordant. Annotations: Qb, Basketmaker III deposits; Qp, Pueblo II deposits.

Place. It is a shallowly buried habitation that consists of a small masonry room block, a kiva, and a midden. The ceramic assemblage indicates occupation during the late Pueblo II period, probably between A.D. 1050 and 1150. It was built into a soil containing transported late Pueblo II ceramics and building stones on cross-laminated tan-gray sand (Figure 2.3) showing westward transport (i.e. a marginal main-channel deposit). This sand is at a depth of 1.8 m below the terrace surface in the cutbank to the south (profile 2). The profile also contains corrugated sherds in two stratigraphically lower buried soil horizons (Figures 1.5 and 2.5), as much as 4.5 m below the level of the Pueblo II-age Anasazi terrace.

Fan-enclosed Sites
Northside fan deposits are dated by ceramics in profiles 1, 2, 3, 5, 6, 15, 24, 29, 35, 36, 37, and 41 (Figure 1.6) and by five architectural sites, all on Kelly Place. The evidence together suggests that northside fan deposits accumulated in Basketmaker III and again in Pueblo II and III periods in the study area.

Dating the Spring Canyon fan (Figure 1.2) relies on CA House (5MT10968), a multicomponent site with Basketmaker III, Pueblo II and Pueblo III occupations. The Basketmaker III component is an intact 25 cm thick horizon of charcoal-stained sediments, charred wood, burned adobe, several edge-shaped sandstone slabs, and Chapin Gray and Chapin Black-on-white sherds, resting on fan deposits. It represents the remains of a pit house that was burned at abandonment. The consequent induration of this deposit apparently caused it to be preserved as the cap of a pinnacle in both the modern erosional episode and a previous one. The older erosional surface separates the pinnacle from mantling Pueblo II fan deposits (Figures 2.7 and 2.8) that filled in the channel between the

Figure 2.8 Annotated photo of fan-channel gravels containing reworked midden debris of Pueblo II age, above an undulating unconformity on Basketmaker III deposits, profile 3. Annotations: Qb, Basketmaker III deposits; Qp, Pueblo II deposits

pinnacle and the main body of the Basketmaker III fan and eventually buried the pinnacle. The Pueblo II deposits contain ceramic fragments against the unconformity (Figure 2.9), and nearby contain a late Pueblo II midden reworked into channel gravels at profile 3 (Figure 2.8). No Pueblo II architecture is apparent. Modern erosion has exhumed the approximate shape of the older pinnacle (Figure 2.6).

A Pueblo III component at CA House consists of a block of six masonry rooms situated in a cluster of boulders near the bedrock cliff, with a kiva and midden on the fan southeast of it. Ceramics indicate an early Pueblo III occupation. Following abandonment, the room block and kiva were filled and mantled by fan deposits.

In summary, CA House shows fan aggradation before or during the Basketmaker III period, a post-Basketmaker III/pre-Pueblo II erosional episode that entrenched the fan, and

a resumption of fan deposition in the Pueblo II and into the Pueblo III periods (Figure 2.5).

Relations at CA house are refined by the nearby Garden site (5MT11739), where interbedded fan and floodplain deposits contain three temporal components (profile 41). Below a thin upper fan deposit are mixed Basketmaker III and early Pueblo II ceramic assemblages in an incipient paleosol on an older fan. An undated cultural horizon occurs about 2 m below this unconformity; it is probably of earlier Basketmaker age. To the north, the upper fan deposits thicken, and contain a dense midden with a ceramic assemblage indicative of early Pueblo II occupation (Figure 1.6) beginning about A.D. 900. Thus early Pueblo II occupation was apparently on an eroded surface of Basketmaker III age.

The Island Site (5MT11738) is in the fan between Park and Settler's canyons (Figure 1.2) on the north side of Kelly Place. It is a multi-

Figure 2.9 Annotated photo of detail of the unconformity revealed by excavation on east side of
pinnacle seen in Figure 2.7. Annotations: Qb,
Basketmaker III deposits; Qp, Pueblo II deposits.

main room block, a midden in the cutbank to
the south, and several low rubble alignments
extending north from the base of the north room
block that appear to be the remains of earlier
structures. The kiva partially overlies an earlier pit structure. All of these components are
set into or on one unit of pink fan sand, and are
buried by another. Architectural detail and
burial assemblages reportedly found within and
under the rooms indicate that portions of the
north room block were constructed prior to
early Pueblo III, whereas other portions were
definitely added in the Pueblo III period. Surface ceramics from around the room blocks and
the midden include a substantial middle to late
Pueblo II assemblage as well as an early Pueblo
III assemblage, suggesting that Sue's Ruin was
founded in Pueblo II, probably by A.D. 1050,
and occupied during early Pueblo III, probably
until A.D. 1225. Occupation may not have been
continuous. Several Basketmaker III and
Pueblo I sherds were also found near the
midden, and hint at earlier occupations in underlying deposits.

Following abandonment of the kiva,
whose roof was removed, fan sediments filled
the depression to a level 40 cm below the top
of the exposed roof-support pilasters. Deposition on this surface is marked by two upward-
fining flood deposits (Figure 2.10) derived from
Cactus Canyon, that draped the kiva basin and
formed dish-shaped clay lenses separated by a
thin band of coarse sediments. These flood episodes are also traceable on a paleo-surface sloping up to the room block. An additional 1.1 to
1.5 m of fan sediments derived from Cactus
Canyon mantle the flood deposits and obscured
the room block, kiva and midden (Figure 2.5).
The occupation at Sue's Ruin thus separates a
lower fan deposit of Pueblo II age or older from
an upper Cactus Canyon-derived fan of Pueblo
III age or younger.

In a cutbank 22 m northeast of Sue's Ruin
(profile 1), the head of the Cactus Canyon fan

component site; a Basketmaker III midden in
lower fan deposits is overlain by a Pueblo III
room block and kiva. The latter structures are
buried by upper fan deposits. The stratigraphy
shows two pulses of fan growth, during
Basketmaker III and again during or after
Pueblo III occupation.

Sue's Ruin (5MT11735) is a multicomponent Pueblo II–Pueblo III habitation located
on the extensive fan east of the mouth of Cactus Canyon (Figure 1.2). The site has been exposed by excavation and reveals a complex
stratigraphic (profile 5) and occupational history. It consists of a surface room block of at
least nine rooms, a later room block southwest
of the first, a kiva 7 m in diameter south of the

Figure 2.10a General view of Sue's Ruin (5MT11735) kiva. Arrow points to contact between ponded flood deposits of Cactus Canyon fan and ~~overlying~~ older cultural material. The uppermost deposits are pink sands also of Cactus Canyon fan.

has been truncated by modern erosion. Below 0.8 m of the upper fan, flood, and cultural deposits of profile 5 (Figure 2.5), the remains of an unusual masonry column are exposed. It now consists of 10 courses of unshaped sandstone blocks that stand 1.8 m high. The column protrudes from sediments above large boulders at the base of the deposit. When first exposed by erosion in the 1970s, the column was near a large sandstone disk, now missing. The function of this feature is unknown. Although no artifacts were associated with the masonry column, large-scale coursed masonry construction such as this generally did not become common until the Pueblo II period. A sparse midden deposit 0.2 to 0.4 m thick separates a lower fan deposit that contains the column from the overlying culturally sterile upper Cactus Canyon fan. Ceramics from this midden date to the late Pueblo II and early Pueblo III periods. A few feet down the arroyo from the column,

Figure 2.10b Detail of excavated southeast wall. Arrow points to contact of silty flood deposits and older cultural material. Scale in cm.

detrital gray ware pottery of Basketmaker III–Pueblo I age occurs in a fan deposit at a depth similar to that of the column base. We think it most probable that the column was built in a pit excavated into a fan of Basketmaker III–Pueblo I age, and subsequently filled by pre-midden fan deposits. Thus, the history of this site is similar to and possibly extends that of nearby Sue's Ruin.

Downstream from Cactus Canyon, George's Ruin (5MT11734) consists of a small room block tucked under an overhang, with a small kiva excavated into adjacent fan deposits. Ceramics recovered in the kiva indicate occupation during the early Pueblo III period, as do ceramics recovered from a horizon correlative with the kiva lip in profile 6. Pink sand of the Cactus Canyon fan fills the kiva and forms an overlying 1.35 m layer. George's Ruin thus separates a lower fan of pre-Pueblo III age from an upper Cactus Canyon fan of Pueblo III age or younger (Figure 2.5).

Surface Sites

Sites on the Anasazi Alluvial Terrace

Sites on exposed alluvial surfaces provide a minimum age for the deposits beneath. Commonly a mixture in artifact ages shows repeated occupation, but generally the age of first settlement can be established. Ceramic assemblages in this context include some from profiles 3, 10, 11, 15, 24, 26, 27, 29, 33, and 36 (Figure 1.6). Three architectural sites are also exposed on the surface of the Anasazi alluvial terrace within the project area. All periods from Basketmaker III through Pueblo III are represented.

Two occupation periods are indicated at the confluence of Goodman and Trail canyons with McElmo Creek. The northeastern map location of composite profile 26 (Figure 1.2) is a surface artifact scatter; no architectural features are visible. Ceramics indicate primary occupation during the late Pueblo II period. A few Pueblo I sherds are also present. The Galloway site is located 50 m to the southwest in and near a cut bank. It is a habitation that contains partial remains of a Pueblo I surface room block and portions of two pit structures exposed in the cut bank. The ceramic assemblage indicates occupation in the late Pueblo I period between A.D. 830 and 880. The Goodman Canyon site is located north of the Galloway site and consists of an extensive surface artifact scatter. Architectural features have been obscured by plowing. The surface ceramic assemblage contains roughly equal percentages of Moccasin Gray and Mancos Gray sherds, an indicator of occupation late into the 800s. These sites demonstrate that the terrace in this area predates the Pueblo I period.

On an alluvial terrace remnant 1 km below the mouth of Goodman Canyon is the Fury site, a slab-lined cist with a scatter of Basketmaker III sherds. Profile 24 at this location also documented Basketmaker III sherds in association with two paleosols about 3 m below the terrace surface. The profile contains interbedded floodplain and northside fan deposits. The stratigraphy suggests that aggradation was followed by terrace stability, all within the Basketmaker III period.

Sites On Bedrock and Southside Fans

Bedrock habitation sites have no direct bearing on the dating of alluvium, but can shed cultural material into the contemporary or later alluvial environment, providing a maximum age. Only three bedrock sites in the study area seemed close enough to alluvium to investigate this possibility. The Graveyard Canyon site (Figure 1.2) is a Pueblo III talus habitation with an associated cliff-top architectural component. The site may be responsible for the introduction of sherds at profiles 33 and 35, and may be related to the checkdam of profile 42. Moqui Point Ruin is located at the mouth of Moqui

Canyon (Figure 1.2), and is a Pueblo III talus room block and kiva with a cliff-top masonry room block. It lacks correlative buried remains (profile 8) probably because the adjacent alluvium is a main channel facies. Castle Rock Pueblo (5MT1825) is a village with 50 to 75 rooms and 10 to 15 kivas (Kuckelman et al. 1991) near the western edge of the study area (Figure 1.2). It provided no datable material in the adjacent alluvial terrace of Anasazi age because of the lack of nearby entrenched exposures.

The surfaces of southside fans contain ceramic scatters at three locations (Figure 1.2)—at the mouth of Jessup Canyon (profile 27), just below Kelly Place (profile 10), and on a bedrock ledge just upstream from the mouth of Sand Canyon (profile 11). All are Basketmaker III in age. They suggest that formation of these surfaces predate Anasazi occupation, and were not affected by later periods of erosion or deposition.

General Geologic Relations

Morpho-chronologic Relations

Buried archaeological sites of Anasazi age are found in association with floodplain deposits and northside fan deposits of the Anasazi terrace. No buried sites were found on southside fans; indeed Basketmaker III sites are commonly found on their upper surfaces, suggesting that most and perhaps all southside fans predate Anasazi occupation. The question of different ages of sediment supply on the two sides of the valley is discussed below.

The Anasazi terrace seems to form a single surface sloping gently westward. However, we find that it actually is a collage of deposits basically of Basketmaker III, Pueblo II, and Pueblo III ages, each composed mostly of interbedded floodplain and northside fan deposits. For each element of this collage, the upper surface seems to be a mostly depositional

rather than erosional surface. The approximate accordance of this upper surface among collage elements is either a coincidence, or it represents an upper bounding surface of aggradation through the A.D. 500 to 1300 portion of the Holocene. We prefer the latter view. Some implications for the progressive formation of the composite terrace are contained in the stratigraphic relations of the two depositional packages, described below.

Stratigraphic Relations

Profiles of as much as 8 m of Anasazi-age alluvium are composed of channel, floodplain, and northside fan deposits. The thickest sections tend to show channel facies at the base, generally grading upward into floodplain deposits, but locally overlain directly by fan deposits. The channel-floodplain association may be represented by as much as 5 m of thickness in which over 40 flood events can be recognized. Fan deposits as thick as 5 m were also observed; they comprise some whole sections near tributary mouths. In some sections they occur toward the top and overlie channel or floodplain deposits. Separation of fan deposits into constituent depositional sequences is possible locally, especially where buried soils, habitation surfaces or other paleo-surfaces, or thin floodplain deposits separate pink sands. Most sections bottom in alluvium, so that relations at the valley floor are unknown.

Pink sands of the northside fans are interbedded with main-channel and floodplain deposits in many sections throughout the study area—most commonly near the mouths of northside tributaries (Figures 1.2, 1.5, and 2.5). Where the sedimentary bodies can be traced, floodplain deposits pinch out northward as the underlying fan surfaces gain elevation (Figures 2.2, 2.4, and 2.5). Thus main-channel floods periodically lapped onto the toes of alluvial fans derived from northside tributaries. The main channel could not have been severely entrenched during the times of such accumulation. Indeed this relation, with the gradational and directional relations described previously between flood deposits and channel deposits, suggests a braided stream in an aggrading valley.

All deposits known to be of Anasazi age share this aggrading relation among channel, floodplain, and fan deposits except the unconformity described below. In-place Anasazi archaeological remains are preferentially in pink sand fan deposits or on the buried surfaces of such fans, and the buried checkdams (profile 4; Figure 2.4) suggest that their agriculture was largely based on them. Other Anasazi sites are on the slightly weathered surfaces of floodplain deposits.

Three sections (profiles 2, 24, and 37) contain multiple buried cultural remains, surmounted on the Anasazi terrace by architectural sites representing the same time period. Intervening sediment ranges from 3.1 to 4.5 m thick, and includes pink fan sand and floodplain deposits. Minimum indicated accumulation rates for these sequences range from 1.5 to 2.5 meters per hundred years. If these growth rates for the period A.D. 500–1300 were representative of the entire Holocene and the whole study area, the valley would have filled to depths of about 100 meters. Clearly no such thick, uniform accumulation occurred. Thus the measured accumulation rates are anomalous, and suggest rapid deposition in restricted depositional sites. The Anasazi apparently followed and inhabited loci of rapid aggradation. Such sites can be linked to Anasazi agriculture at profile 4 and to Anasazi habitation throughout Kelly Place (Figure 2.5) and profiles 24 and 37 (Figure 1.5). Based on the common association of habitation sites with incipient paleosols in rapidly aggrading environments, the Anasazi need for flood protection was modest, but the problem was minimized by choosing less vulnerable sites.

An unconformity separates deposits of the Anasazi terrace into two sequences. The unconformity is described below with depositional packages of different ages.

Areal Relations

Broadly speaking, alluvium of Basketmaker III age forms the Anasazi terrace in much of the eastern part of the study area, whereas deposits of Pueblo III age form much of the east-central portion (Figures 1.2 and 1.5). Near Kelly Place, the Anasazi terrace is underlain mostly by alluvium of Pueblo II age, draped unconformably over deposits of Basketmaker III age, and overlain along the northern valley margin by small fans of Pueblo III or younger age (Figure 2.5). In the westernmost part of the area, the age of deposits below the Anasazi terrace is not well known, but appears to be mostly Pueblo II and Pueblo III. Southside fans in the study area are either older deposits, predating Basketmaker III, or of unknown age. Two depositional packages are described below.

Broad floodplains of Anasazi age are preserved in only a few stretches of the valley in the study area (Figure 1.2). Locally these are as wide as 500 m. Near the mouths of Sand and Goodman canyons, large northside fans occupied much of the valley width and constricted the channel against the southern valley margin. In a few other areas, such as Kelly Place where the total valley width was limiting, smaller fans constricted the channel. Constriction due to older southside fans apparently occurred in only one reach downstream of Kelly Place, between profiles 7 and 10. As a result of the asymmetry of constriction across the valley in Anasazi time, the channel was forced against the south side of the valley in most reaches, as shown by the distribution of channel-floodplain deposits (Figure 1.2). Channel-facies deposits of probable Anasazi age were found on the northern margin of the valley in only a few places (such as profile 8).

Where the channel was constricted, channel- or intermediate-facies main-drainage deposits are finely interbedded with distal pink-sand fan deposits (Figure 2.3), as if the fans disgorged directly into the main channel. The distorted shape of the Anasazi-age fan of Sand Canyon (Figure 1.2) reflects the interference of channel and fan in a constricted valley.

A sketchy history of valley constriction can be compiled from the distribution of deposits of different ages. During the entire Anasazi period from Basketmaker III time onward, the valley was constricted and pressed against the south side in the eastern end of the study area as far downstream as profile 24. A reach downstream from Kelly Place (from profiles 7 to 10) was also constricted during the entire period. In the Pueblo II period the valley was pressed to the south at Kelly Place. The area of the mouth of Sand Canyon was similarly constricted at some time from Pueblo II to Pueblo III. Evidence of additional constrictions may have been eroded, so conclusions based on changes of constriction distribution must be made with care.

The local rapid growth of northside fans in the Anasazi period, when southside fans were limited or quiescent, is well-established but puzzling. Southside tributaries must be capable of supplying debris at a rate commensurate with northside tributaries — their drainage basins are comparable, relief is great, and they had earlier deposited fans of considerable size. It is probably the northside fans that are anomalous in this time period, as noted above. If the northside fans did indeed grow at an anomalous rate during the Anasazi period, the coincidence suggests the possibility that man's agricultural practices—impounding sediment in the study area and disturbing natural cover in the mesa-top headwaters of northside drainages—enhanced the deposition rate.

Depositional Packages

Alluvium of the Anasazi terrace can be divided into two depositional packages, and the younger can be further subdivided based on age. The older package, mostly of Basketmaker III age, is separated from the younger by an unconformity. In the younger package, deposits of Pueblo II age are overlain and bordered on the east in imbricate fashion by deposits of Pueblo III age. Locally, northside fans of Pueblo III or later age came to rest on the Pueblo II portion. Relations of deposits of varying age are shown diagrammatically as Figure 2.11.

Deposits of Basketmaker III age are best developed at profile 24. A thick section of floodplain and northside fan deposits there contains two paleosols bearing Basketmaker III ceramics, and the section is surmounted by Basketmaker III architecture. Similar deposits at profile 26 are surmounted by a Pueblo I village. We speculate that deposits of Pueblo I age, probably no longer preserved, were originally part of this depositional package at the eastern end of the study area (Figure 2.11), because elsewhere in the study area, habitation implies nearby deposition. Had the upstream stretch of valley already been entrenched, the tributary fans would have been entrenched also, and it is hard to imagine a floodwater agricultural base for the community.

An unconformity separates the Basketmaker III deposits from younger deposits. In the middle to eastern parts of the study area, where the Basketmaker III package is most widely distributed, the unconformity is overlain by deposits of Pueblo III age. The best exposure of the unconformity in this eastern portion is at site 32, where the two sequences, each consisting of interbedded floodplain and northside fan deposits, are separated by an erosion surface. Toward the south this surface is steep, locally overhanging (Figure 2.6). Toward the north it dips very gently southward and in-

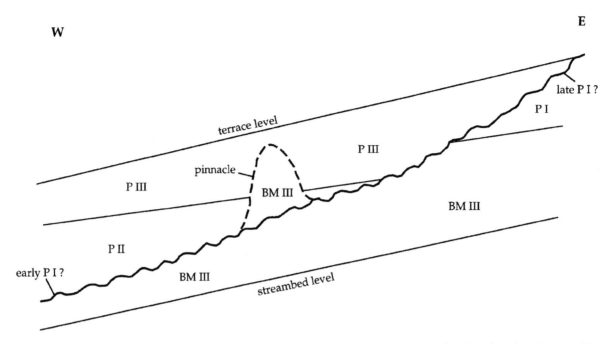

Figure 2.11 Longitudinal diagram of depositional packages relative to the unconformity, showing the probable diachronous nature of the unconformity and migration of depositional lobes. The annotations are abbreviations of time divisions from Figure 1.3.

tersects the terrace surface near the shallowly-buried firepit. Nearby, locality 42 records local non-accordance of the terrace surfaces formed on deposits above and below this unconformity.

On Kelly Place, erosional remnants of Basketmaker III deposits are surrounded and overlain by deposits of Pueblo II and Pueblo III age. The unconformity shows relief of about 3 m (Figure 2.7) and is locally almost vertical, so that a badland topography on Basketmaker III deposits is buried under the Anasazi terrace, mostly by Pueblo II deposits (Figures 2.7 and 2.8). Two segments of the unconformity surface are described above with CA House and the Garden site. Profiles 1, 3, and 41 also contain the unconformity (Figure 2.5). Deposits both above and below the unconformity are pink sand fan deposits, with thin greenish mudflows. The unconformity is most commonly marked by slight color changes, a gravel layer, and in some profiles by a mixed ceramic assemblage. The unconformity is visible along the entire cut bank between Spring Canyon and Garden Draw as a gently sloping to steeply undulating contact between an underlying zone of compact pink sand and less compact overlying fan and fan-channel deposits (Figure 2.8).

Ceramic remains above and below the unconformity bracket its age between A.D. 700–750 and 930 at Kelly Place, but near the mouth of Goodman Canyon it is apparently younger. When all the pertinent ceramic assemblages are plotted along the drainage, they show that the unconformity becomes younger to the east (Figure 1.6). In many of the profiles from which the ceramics come, this gap corresponds to the unconformity described above.

Plots of age constraints on the unconformity itself also suggest diachronous development (Figure 2.12). The apparent diachroneity of the unconformity suggests upstream migration of a locus of entrenchment or the overprinting of one erosional event by another.

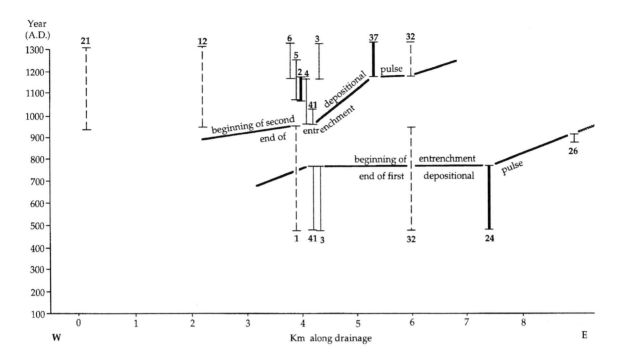

Figure 2.12 Graph of age vs. position of aggradation and entrenchment. Profile numbers and position from Figure 1.5, ages of ceramic assemblages in depositional context from Figures 1.3 and 1.6. Vertical bars show age ranges: dashed bars indicate detrital assemblage (may be younger); bold bars indicate multiple habitation levels within the age range shown.

Deposits of Pueblo II age may form the entire exposed thickness of the Anasazi terrace in much of the western part of the study area. In its westernmost parts, however, this package is poorly dated. The best control is on Kelly Place where at profile 2 at least 3.3 m of interbedded floodplain and northside fan deposits are of Pueblo II age (Figure 2.5). These deposits form the central horizontal parts of the Anasazi terrace on Kelly Place but rise slightly to the north as northside fans of the same age. Greenish Morrison-derived mudflows drape these fan surfaces, but are interbedded with fan and floodplain deposits of Pueblo II age as in profile 2.

A complex of small fans from northside tributaries on Kelly Place are of Pueblo III and later age. It is these fans that form the apices of the Anasazi terrace into Cactus, Settler's, Park, and Spring canyons, from which their material was derived. The fan deposits are commonly as thin as 2 m, but may be thicker where the channels had entrenched, as at the mouth of Cactus Canyon (Figure 2.5).

A summary of relations on Kelly Place is provided by Figure 2.5. An irregular unconformity left Basketmaker III deposits at the surface of the Anasazi terrace in only one area, but eroded remnants occur at depth along the northern margin of the valley. Deposits of Pueblo II age overlie this surface in most of the area, but are best exposed toward the south where they are dominated by floodplain deposits. Northside fans of Pueblo II age grew into this southern area, as shown by the buried checkdam and by the mantling green mudflows. Deposits of Pueblo III age and later consist of pink-sand fans derived from canyons on the north side of the valley, which extended only part way across the older Pueblo II surface.

However, the main volume of Pueblo III deposits form a sequence above the unconformity east of Kelly Place. These deposits are well represented from profile 37 upstream to profile 30. Apparently they accumulated above Pueblo II deposits conformably, but direct evidence is lacking. At profile 37, they consist of over 4 m of interbedded floodplain and northside fan deposits. The eastern margin of the Pueblo III deposits is against the unconformity. In the area of locality 32, Pueblo III deposits form sequences southward of the Basketmaker III deposits, but graded to the same upper surface (Figure 2.6). Deposits of Pueblo III age apparently form a younger terrace at the same level near profile 30, but probable Pueblo III deposits at profile 42 are graded to a lower surface.

Thus, main-valley deposits of Pueblo II age are overlain, probably conformably, by Pueblo III deposits in overlapping fashion, such that the younger deposits are found to the east. The locus of deposition must have shifted in that direction (Figure 2.11).

Summary

Apparently, deposits of Basketmaker III age once filled the valley to the present level of the Anasazi terrace; the evidence is good between Kelly Place and Goodman Canyon but lacking below Kelly Place. These deposits were removed by erosion in approximately the Pueblo I period in most areas. Upstream progression of the locus of entrenchment (Figures 1.6, 2.11, and 2.12) is suggested by the apparent older age of the unconformity on Kelly Place (profile 41 area) than at the mouth of Goodman Canyon (profile 26 area). Following entrenchment, the valley began to backfill to the original level, beginning at the downstream end of the study area with floodplain and fan deposits of early Pueblo II age. The upstream end of the study area may have still been eroding at this time (Figures 2.11 and 2.12). As the depositional lobe moved upstream, early Pueblo III deposits lapped onto the Pueblo II deposits eastward to fill much of the relief remaining from erosion. The diachronous nature of both aggradation and entrenchment events are shown by Figure 2.12, which converts the ceramic information of Figure 1.6 into the relation between age and position of these events.

An alternative explanation of Figures 1.6 and 2.12 might be that two distinct erosional episodes had different loci or different gradients. However, we prefer the migration of a single erosional locus, at least as far upstream as profile 32, because the migration of the subsequent depositional lobe in overlapping manner, with no apparent internal unconformities, suggests the infilling of a single physiographic trough.

Chapter Three

Area History

Geomorphic History

In Basketmaker III time, the valley was filling with braided-facies channel-floodplain deposits and northside fans that are remarkably similar to those that formed during the later Pueblo II-Pueblo III period. The upper levels and gradient of the two sets of deposits are about the same (Figures 1.5 and 2.6), indicating that baselevel and other controls were the same for the two depositional stages. This similarity can be contrasted with the two stages of deposition that produced the younger inset terraces and modern deposits, which record approximately the same gradient but lower terrace levels and a meandering regime. The locus of deposition was probably migrating upstream from Basketmaker III into Pueblo I time, based on the eastward shift of settlement during this period.

The unconformity between deposits of Basketmaker III and Pueblo II ages suggests severe entrenchment, especially in Pueblo I time. Most exposures of this surface show considerable relief, steep to undulating slopes, and local cut-banks suggestive of local badland topography and meandering stream regime during the period of erosion. Entrenchment apparently migrated upstream, based on the probable older age of the unconformity toward the west (Figures 1.6, 2.11, and 2.12).

Valley aggradation began again in the early Pueblo II period, with significant accumulation mostly or only in the downstream end of the study area. Upstream as far as Kelly Place, the valley had aggraded to approximately its former extent by the end of Pueblo II time

(Figures 1.5, 2.5, and 2.7). The apparent gradient of this valley segment at this time was gentle. From the Huddleston site eastward to the upstream end of the area, erosion surfaces had apparently filled in only slightly (as at profile 42).

During Pueblo III time, aggradation generally filled in the remaining valley-bottom erosion surfaces in the upstream end of the study area to produce the Anasazi terrace. Small northside fans continued to shape the Anasazi terrace in the central parts of the area by building on the previously constructed Pueblo II surface.

The geomorphic status of the study area in each period is shown schematically in Figure 3.1. Three loci of aggradation and entrenchment may have traversed the study area in the Anasazi period (Figures 1.6, 2.11, and 2.12). Rather weak evidence suggests the passage of a locus of aggradation through the study area from Basketmaker III probably into Pueblo I time. Stronger evidence suggests that the locus of subsequent entrenchment moved upstream mostly in Pueblo I time. Similarly, entrenchment was followed by a pulse of renewed aggradation, which firm evidence shows to have travelled upstream in Pueblo II–III time. Even within the study area, these events probably overlapped in time. The implied upstream migration rate for each of the three events, about 20 m per year, is actually a minimum because available dates merely bracket the events.

A progression of apparent valley gradients can also be discerned from the sections (Figures 1.5, 2.5, and 2.11). Headward parts of entrenched segments were steeper than the

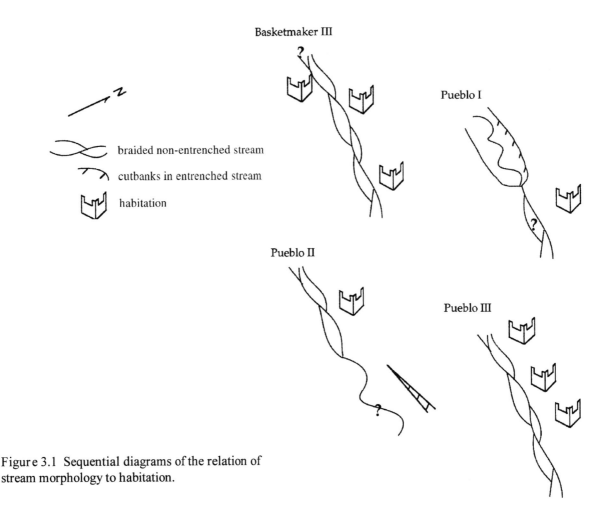

Figure 3.1 Sequential diagrams of the relation of stream morphology to habitation.

overall envelope of the Anasazi terrace, whereas the preserved (upstream) ends of aggrading segments had gradients gentler than the average (Figure 3.2).

Habitation History

The archaeological data when aggregated by time period give a habitation history that further constrains environmental change and drainage evolution.

Basketmaker III

Remains of Basketmaker III age occur on both sides of the valley and throughout the study area (Figure 1.6). The only definite evidence of residential architecture is the lower component at CA House on Kelly Place, but substantial artifact scatters and middens elsewhere in the study area indicate other habitations or intensively utilized special-use sites. Two sites (profiles 24 and 41) consist of both buried and surface components, suggestive of continuous or repeated use.

The Basketmaker III valley-bottom settlement distribution in McElmo Canyon reflects the broader settlement pattern for the canyons, benches, and mesas to the north (Adler 1992; Adler and Metcalf 1991; Fetterman and Honeycutt 1987; Gleichman and Gleichman 1992; Van West et al. 1987). There Basketmaker III settlements and special use sites are generally associated with the best available

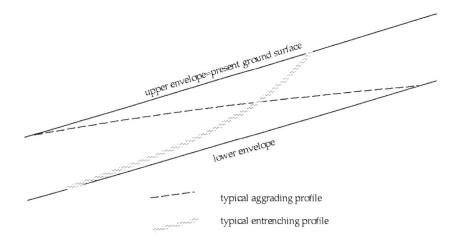

upper envelope=present ground surface

lower envelope

- - - -   typical aggrading profile

typical entrenching profile

Figure 3.2 Diagram of envelope of Anasazi-age deposits showing the relations of valley gradients at different periods. An example of the aggrading profile is the Pueblo II–Pueblo III contact. An example of the entrenching profile is the Pueblo I unconformity. Both the Basketmaker III and Pueblo III periods provide examples of the upper envelope.

agricultural lands. The settlement pattern suggests productive agriculture, apparently related in large part to aggradation in the valley bottom over most of the study area.

Pueblo I

In contrast to the pattern in Basketmaker III, occupation during Pueblo I was apparently limited to the upstream end of the study area (Figure 1.6), where a community grew between A.D. 830–880 on the broad alluvial fans at the confluence of Goodman and Trail canyons with the main drainage. As McElmo Creek was pressed to the south side of its valley by these fans, agriculture was probably on aggrading portions of these fans, on narrow aggrading valley segments above or below the fans, and in Goodman and Trail canyons. We hypothesize that the lack of Pueblo I settlement downstream of this settlement locus is attributable to poor agricultural potential on the fans and floodplains downvalley where the system was entrenching. Apparently, entrenchment did not reach the Goodman Canyon Pueblo I community until later, based on the evolution pattern

of this fluvial system (Figure 2.12) and Anasazi agricultural practices in the other time periods.

Pueblo II

The Pueblo II period saw rapid aggradation in the western and central parts of the study area, as the braided stream deposited floodplain sediments onto the toes of aggrading northside fans. The Anasazi clearly were not avoiding the loci of rapid aggradation; indeed, their water control features indicate that their agriculture relied largely on aggrading distal northside fans where floodwater fields were developed. The quiescent southside fans were apparently not occupied.

Timing of the Pueblo II resettlement of the western and central study area can be placed in the early 900's, based on the ceramic assemblage from the Garden Site. Occupation continued through Pueblo II at Kelly Place, where the floodplain and northside fans continued to aggrade. In late Pueblo II there may have been a lull in floodplain deposition, as the Anasazi established Earbob House on the floodplain in a position fairly close to McElmo Creek, which at this time was pressed to the south side of the valley by the growth of northside fans. The valley segment above Kelly Place appears to have been little-used during the Pueblo II period, suggesting that the area was still entrenched (Figure 3.1).

In adjacent uplands, population increased on mesas in the Pueblo II period (Adler 1992; Van West et al. 1987). The intermediate benches and canyons were little-utilized (Adler and Metcalf 1991; Gleichman and Gleichman 1992).

Pueblo III

The loci of rapid aggradation shifted in Pueblo III time toward the eastern end of the study area and to the northern fringe of the Anasazi terrace, where pink-sand fans continued to grow over the older Pueblo II surface. Pueblo III settlement extended accordingly, again favoring active depositional environments. The quiescent southern side of the valley bottom was apparently not occupied. During the Pueblo III period, a community of four unit pueblos grew on northside fans at Kelly Place. Up-

stream, the Huddleston site was built on the valley fringe, and talus slope- and cliff-edge settlements were established at Moqui Point and the mouth of Graveyard Canyon. Down-canyon, other unit pueblos and Castle Rock Pueblo were settled (Kuckelman et al. 1991). The Pueblo III period was the time of greatest Anasazi population in the adjacent uplands (Adler 1992; Van West et al. 1987), in the intermediate canyons and benches (Adler and Metcalf 1991; Gleichman and Gleichman 1992), and apparently on the valley bottom.

Probably during the first half of the thirteenth century, the Kelly Place community and the Huddleston site were abandoned. However, following these abandonments all of the northside fans continued to aggrade, an indication that agricultural potential was still high, and by inference not a cause for abandonment. Local abandonment probably reflects an overall population aggregation trend throughout the region at that time (Lipe and Lekson 1990). Our data on the initiation of subsequent entrenchment is insufficient to relate it to habitation history.

Chapter Four

Geomorphic Model and Archaeological Implications

A Depositional-Geomorphic Model

Our evidence suggests that both depositional and erosional events in the study area were diachronous, migrating upstream at rates of about 20 m per year or more, but resolvable within the limits of archaeological dating. Here we explore some implications of our depositional-geomorphic framework.

Upstream shifts in the loci of entrenchment and aggradation similar to those of the study area have been observed in modern fluvial systems and flumes. At any given time, the locus of entrenchment occupies only portions of a valley segment, with each segment tending to migrate upstream (Cooke and Reeves 1976). The increased sediment yield causes downstream aggradation, whose locus migrates upstream behind the locus of entrenchment ("complex response" of Schumm (1973; see Schumm et al. 1984, 1987). At any given point, sediment load of the stream varies from decade to decade even at constant discharge rates as the loci of sediment storage migrate (Gellis et al. 1991).

Stratigraphic records consistent with these variations have been observed in Holocene fluvial deposits elsewhere in the southwestern United States. R. J. Weldon (in Bull 1991: Figures 4.33 to 4.39) and Packard (1974) documented upstream migration patterns of loci of erosion and deposition similar to Figures 2.11 and 2.12 of this study. Our minimum average migration rate of 20 m per year falls between

greater values observed in some modern drainages and the average rate determined by Weldon, about 2 m per year. The apparent difference between migration rates determined stratigraphically and those determined by direct observation may be due to more potent anthropogenic effects in the historic period, or erratic fluctuations of the system which are integrated in the stratigraphic record.

Some models treat climate-induced water-table fluctuation as an independent variable that drives regional simultaneous entrenchment (cf. Karlstrom 1988). These seem not to be supported by studies of modern fluvial systems. The variables that apparently determine entrenchment thresholds are discharge, width, gradient, bottom cohesion, and sediment load (Schumm et al. 1984). If the threshold is exceeded, entrenchment proceeds up-valley, at rates determined in part by bottom cohesion. Discharge is related to climate, but the most common discharge-related effect on entrenchment is periodic flooding, both in the modern record (Cooke and Reeves 1976; Hereford and Webb 1992; Webb and Baker 1987) and the Holocene stratigraphic record (Love 1979, 1983a, 1983b; Webb 1985).

Environmental reconstructions for the Anasazi (D'Arrigo and Jacoby 1991; Dean 1988) and historic (Balling and Wells 1990; Hereford and Webb 1992; Leopold 1951) periods suggest that times of entrenchment are also those of high rainfall variability. In such conditions, periods of low rainfall and sparse

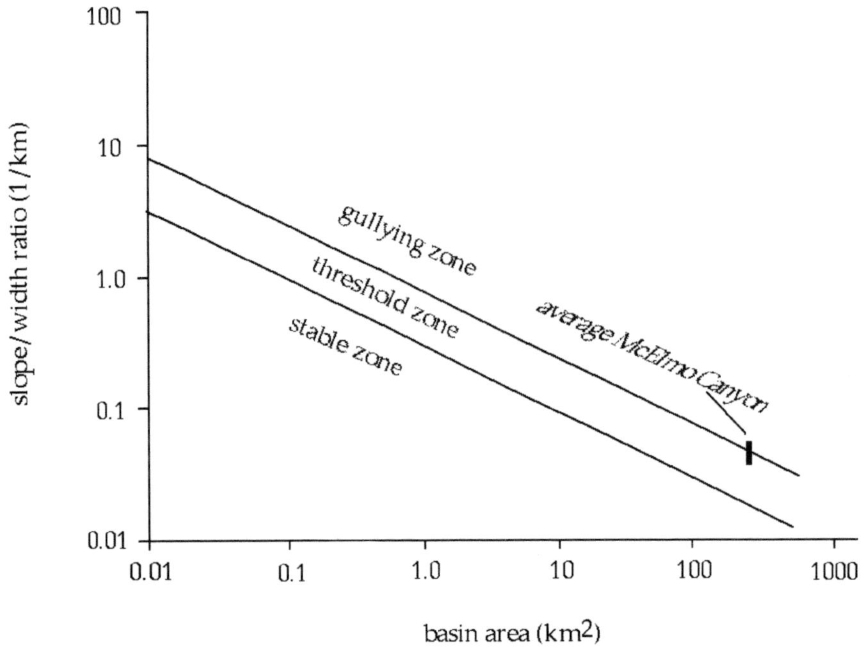

Figure 4.1 Relation of McElmo Canyon hydraulic conditions to entrenchment thresholds. The graph of slope-width ratio versus basin area, and fields thereon, is based on Schumm et al. (1984).

vegetation (low bottom cohesion) are juxtaposed with those of high rainfall and high discharge (rapid erosion). McElmo and similar canyons inherently approach entrenchment thresholds defined by other drainage variables (Figure 4.1), so that rainfall variability and resultant flooding may easily correspond with entrenchment.

The Anasazi, themselves, may have triggered entrenchment in McElmo Canyon by any of several activities: 1) Agricultural activities may have increased sediment supply and thus the size of northside fans, thereby constricting and steepening the main channel; 2) Clearing for floodwater agriculture may have decreased bottom cohesion; and 3) Sediment impoundment behind water-control features on fans may have decreased sediment load. Prior to the Pueblo II period, however, such anthropogenic effects were probably minimal.

The diachronous nature of sediment accumulation and stream entrenchment in the study area presents us with a dilemma. On the one hand, our stratigraphic sequence conforms generally to those of the larger region (Figure 1.4), in the sense that our stratigraphic package-

ages correspond to time envelopes of accumulation in other drainages. On the other hand, the diachronous events in our small study area would suggest marked diachroneity within the McElmo drainage as a whole, and forbid detailed correlation with other drainages. How then can regional aggregation of local diachronous events produce a regional chronostratigraphic sequence?

The nature of the evidence for the regional sequence provides a clue (Figure 1.4). We note that in individual sections, dating constraints permit diachronous development and in some cases require it, even within the type area near Black Mesa. Age variations of about 200 years appear to be quite common. Such age variations of features within the sediments of Anasazi age are unclear because the chronology depends on correlation of soils whose age uncertainty is typically about 200 years. Thus we consider the regional chronostratigraphic sequence a set of time envelopes for erosion and deposition, whose boundaries vary by about 200 years within and between areas.

The time envelopes must be controlled by regional events. We would agree with other investigators that climate change is probably the main factor, as no regional baselevel change is known in the pertinent time period, and the time period available is too slight for baselevel change to affect each bedrock-locked stream reach. However, we would add regional land-use change by the Anasazi themselves as a contributing factor consistent with the findings of this study and those of nearby areas (Betancourt et al. 1983; Vivian 1974; Winter 1976, 1977).

Within the regional time envelopes, diachronous events in each drainage probably follow the sequence described in this study and elsewhere. Bedrock-locked reaches of each drainage may evolve simultaneously, such that similarly situated stretches of adjacent drainages, or similar segments of the same drainage, are in similar stages of evolution. Thus some apparently close correlations can evolve.

Relations Among Habitation, Environment, and Depositional Regime

Adaptation of Habitation to the Depositional Regime

The history of Anasazi habitation on McElmo Canyon floodlands is clearly controlled by the depositional environment. We see two fundamental and related behavioral responses that allowed the Anasazi to utilize this dynamic environment—agricultural adaptation and settlement siting. These two responses in turn determine another shifting of settlement location. All these adaptations are best understood in their depositional contexts.

Agriculture

The buried Pueblo II checkdam at profile 4 indicates an agriculture based on controlling floodwaters on aggrading alluvial fans (Figure 2.4), and the orientation of several other Anasazi checkdams in and near the study area sup-

ports the picture of agriculture on northside fans using floodwaters of those fans. The checkdam of profile 42 demonstrates that some agriculture was also based on the impoundment of water and sediment in distal margins of the main-channel floodplain. The main type of agriculture indicated is one recorded in modern pueblo societies, sometimes called ak chin farming (Hack 1942). Checkdams are used partly for soil retention and partly for distribution of runoff over the fan surface. Vivian (1974) reported similar agricultural practices during Pueblo II at Chaco Canyon, and Winter (1976, 1977) has documented fan and floodplain agricultural features at nearby Hovenweep. At Kelly Place, where our evidence is best, runoff from about 2 square kilometers of steep bedrock slopes is naturally funneled onto a fan system of about 0.25 square kilometers, where checkdams would be sufficient for distribution.

This system requires an actively aggrading fan, as checkdams cannot distribute water from an entrenched channel. An aggrading fan implies in turn a braided, aggrading main channel, because 1) an entrenched main channel leads to entrenchment of its tributaries, and 2) a meandering main channel periodically cuts the toe of its side fans, steepening their gradients and causing entrenchment. This hypothesized association of aggrading fans with adjacent aggrading braided channels is consistent with the observed interbedding of floodplain and fan-toe deposits in sites associated with Anasazi agriculture, as well as the more distant gradations between channel and floodplain deposits of the same age. It is also consistent with subsidiary floodwater agriculture on distal margins of the floodplain.

Settlement Siting

The common occurrence in the study area of Anasazi dwellings in northside fan deposits, coupled with the scarcity of architectural remains in valley segments that were not concurrently aggrading, suggests that habitation as well as agriculture was focused primarily on those northside fans that were actively aggrading. However, aggrading valley floors and growing fans are unstable living surfaces due to periodic flooding and saturated substrates.

The Anasazi dealt with the inherent gamble of unstable living surfaces mostly by settling on the less-active parts of aggrading systems. These included northside alluvial fans (CA House, the Island site, Sue's Ruin and George's Ruin), old terrace remnants on the valley flank (the Garden and Huddleston sites), on valley edge talus and bedrock locations (Moqui Point and the Graveyard Canyon site), and on inactive parts of the floodplain (i.e., on incipient soils as at Earbob House). In this way they were able to maintain claim to highly desirable agricultural lands by building on relatively stable landforms in the immediate vicinity of the fields. Investment in these residential and agricultural facilities was clearly at risk due to flooding, as shown by the many buried sites in the study area. However, the potential benefit must have outweighed this risk, for they continued to invest in such facilities for generations.

Shifting Settlement Location

Most of the shifting of Anasazi habitation observed in the study area, tracking the locus of rapid valley aggradation, is a consequence of the type of agriculture being practiced. As aggradation pulses moved upstream, so did settlements. This is clearest for the early and middle Pueblo II and early Pueblo III periods, for which upstream-imbricated sequences of interbedded fan and floodplain deposits enclose multiple habitation surfaces (Figure 1.5). Settlements coeval with entrenchment in other valley segments are not known. Pueblo I settlement at the mouth of Goodman Canyon could be an example, but is more readily explained by later erosion of the coeval aggradational package.

Some settlement shifting in Pueblo III time has no obvious relation to floodland conditions. For example, the Kelly Place sites were abandoned when adjacent northside fans were still aggrading. This shift was probably in response to cultural factors that led to population aggregation throughout the region at that time (Lipe and Lekson 1990).

Relation of Entrenchment to Habitation

The relation of arroyo incision to habitation and abandonment has long been of interest in studies of the Holocene in the southwestern U.S. (Bryan 1941; Euler et al. 1979; Hack 1942; Karlstrom 1988). This study examines the mutual stratigraphy of habitation and depositional-geomorphic evolution in an area where the relation is sensitive to entrenchment. We find that entrenchment is of great local importance to habitation patterns, but because entrenchment is diachronous, its effects can be mitigated or compensated by migration along the drainage system.

Two specific vignettes of this study suggest the importance of entrenchment for site but not regional abandonment: 1) the severe Pueblo I entrenchment episode produced local and perhaps diachronous abandonment of the valley bottom in the entrenched segment, but was eventually followed by diachronous recolonization following the locus of aggradation, and 2) the Kelly Place Pueblo III community was abandoned as part of a regional event, in spite of local fan aggradation that permitted continued agriculture.

Thus entrenchment need not cause abandonment of the entire valley bottom, much less the whole region. Only where entrenchment can be shown to be a simultaneous and widespread regional condition can it form a legitimate hypothesis for explaining abandonment.

The Floodlands as a Habitation Environment

Our view of Anasazi adaptations to the aggrading floodland environment of McElmo Canyon contrasts somewhat with current regional models, but not as much as one might infer from the literature. Dean et al. (1985; elaborated in Gumerman 1988), in a paper correlating low- and high- frequency environmental variability of the region with Anasazi behavioral response, propose a model of population movement into uplands during periods of aggradation and into the valleys during periods of degradation (Dean et al. 1985: 547; see also Plog et al. 1988: 261 and table 8.1).

The reasons given for this behavior are avoidance of "saturated or unstable ground surfaces on floodplains", which would have provided poor construction surfaces (Dean et al. 1985: 547; Plog et al. 1988: 261–263), and an assumed coupling of aggradation with increased precipitation (Karlstrom 1988: 51), such that dryland or rainfall farming in the uplands would have been feasible (and less risky than on the floodplains). Reasons for movement back into the lowlands during periods of arroyo incision are not made clear; little floodwater land is available in incised valleys.

However, Jeff Dean (written communication, 1996) tells us that valley margins rather than true uplands were meant by these authors. Thus we differ only in suggesting that settlement followed aggradation as closely as possible without inundation or burial.

We find evidence of migration of the loci of aggradation and degradation within our study area, which permitted an adaptive local Anasazi strategy, apparently practised through much of Anasazi time, that 1) concentrated agriculture on fans and margins of floodplains in aggrading valley segments, 2) sited settlements on the most stable available landforms adjacent to the fields, and 3) shifted settlements to exploit the best available floodwater lands. We note that any such relation depends on agricultural and cultural practices that may be local and would propose that our results may be applicable only to the Mesa Verde Anasazi.

Elsewhere in the southwestern United States, Waters (1988) found relations like ours among Hohokam records in southern Arizona, whereas Love (1983b) and Orcutt (1991) found various relations in northwestern New Mexico. The disparities suggest that the modelling of migration and mobility requires a better understanding of valley evolution and floodwater agricultural-cultural practices than is generally available. The requisite data have been acquired slowly because the record is mostly buried, the pertinent lands are mostly private, and most research is focused on the uplands.

Our study also suggests that valley-bottom agriculture was a significant component of Anasazi subsistence, but a more regional approach is needed to verify this suggestion. The study of Schlanger (1988), which addressed upland-lowland population shifts in the context of the elevation-controlled farmbelt model of Petersen (1988), is useful for this purpose.

Schlanger examined population movements along the great slope between Dolores (high and to the east) through Woods Canyon to Mockingbird Mesa (low and to the west). Schlanger found the farmbelt model adequate to explain population movements for certain periods, but not others. For example, in Schlanger's (1988: 756) period 7.4 (A.D. 1175–1250; Pueblo III), extended drought rendered her entire area unsuitable for rainfall farming except on the highest eastern mesas, where cold temperatures limited growing season length. Yet Mockingbird Mesa and Woods Canyon showed their highest population levels at this time (Schlanger 1988: 786), whereas the Dolores area was abandoned. Schlanger suggests the agricultural intensification strategies of Winter

(1976, 1977) in the adjoining floodwater drainage to explain the anomaly.

Our results and our view of drainage evolution can be used to enlarge Schlanger's (1988) conclusion. Woods Canyon and Mockingbird Mesa are low-altitude uplands that adjoin headwater segments of large floodlands, which during the Pueblo III period would have been aggrading (by analogy with our study area). Schlanger's population anomaly can be explained as an integrated Anasazi agricultural strategy that compressed population along the canyon-rim interface between upland and floodland environments, where both environments could be farmed most effectively. Population concentrations in other areas would be prevented in this strategy not by farmbelt elevation but by the availability of aggrading floodlands. This example, while merely hypothetical, suggests a bimodal approach to Anasazi subsistence that may be widely applicable.

Where upland farmbelts and floodlands were available, both may have been required for successful Anasazi agriculture in at least some time periods. The productivity of the former is defined by elevation (through temperature and rainfall), whereas the latter is defined by local drainage evolution. The two factors change with time, but in different ways and probably not in concert, so that permissive belts for each can be adjacent only in a few places, which become temporary population centers. This hypothesis of Anasazi strategy must be regarded as largely untested, because so little is known about the floodland component of Anasazi activity. However, it is clear that change in both the upland and floodland environments must be tracked in future research.

References Cited

Adler, Michael A.

    1992   The Upland Survey. In The Sand Canyon Archaeological Project, A Progress Report, edited by W. D. Lipe, pp. 11–24. Occasional Paper 2. Crow Canyon Archaeological Center, Cortez, Colorado.

Adler, Michael A., and Merripat Metcalf

    1991   Draft Report on Archaeological Survey of Lower East Rock and Sand Canyons, Montezuma County, Colorado. Crow Canyon Archaeological Center report to Bureau of Land Management, San Juan Resource Area, Durango, Colorado.

Balling, Robert C., Jr. and Stephen G. Wells,

    1990   Historical Rainfall Patterns and Arroyo Activity within the Zuni River Drainage Basin, New Mexico. Annals of the Association of American Geographers 80:603–617).

Betancourt, Julio L., Paul S. Martin, and T. R. Van Devendter

    1983   Fossil Packrat Middens from Chaco Canyon, New Mexico: Cultural and Ecological Significance in Chaco Canyon Country. In American Geomorphological Field Group 1983 Guidebook, edited by S. G. Wells, D. W. Love, and T. W. Gardner, pp. 207–218. American Geomorphological Field Group.

Birkeland, Peter W., M. N. Machette, and K. M. Haller

    1991   Soils as a Tool for Applied Quaternary Geology. Miscellaneous Publication 91–3. Utah Geological and Mineral Survey.

Blinman, Eric

    1986   Additive Technologies Group Final Report. In Dolores Archaeological Program: Final Synthetic Report, compiled by David A. Breternitz, Christine K. Robinson, and G. Timothy Gross, pp. 53–101. Bureau of Reclamation, Engineering and Research Center, Denver.

Blinman, Eric, and C. Dean Wilson

    1989   Mesa Verde Region Ceramic Types. New Mexico Archaeological Council, Albuquerque.

Breternitz, David A., Arthur H. Rohn, and Elizabeth A. Morris, compilers

    1974   Prehistoric Ceramics of the Mesa Verde Region. Ceramic Series 5. Museum of Northern Arizona, Flagstaff.

Bryan, Kirk

    1941   Precolumbian Agriculture in the Southwest as Conditioned by Periods of Alluviation. Annals of the Association of American Geographers 31(4):219–242.

    1954   The Geology of Chaco Canyon, New Mexico, in Relation to the Life and Remains of the Prehistoric Peoples of Pueblo Bonito. Miscellaneous Collections Vol. 122. Smithsonian Institution, Washington, D.C.

Bull, William B.

    1991   Geomorphic Responses to Climatic Change. Oxford University Press, New York.

Christenson, Gary E.

    1985   Quaternary Geology of the Montezuma Creek–Lower Recapture Creek Area, San Juan County, Utah. Utah Geological and Mineral Survey Special Studies 64:3–31.

Cooke, R. U., and R. W. Reeves

    1976   Arroyos and Environmental Change in the American Southwest. Clarendon Press, Oxford.

Cordell, Linda S.

    1984   Prehistory of the Southwest. Academic Press, New York.

D'Arrigo, Rosanna D., and Gordon C. Jacoby

    1991   A 1000-year Record of Winter Precipitation from Northwestern New Mexico, USA: A Reconstruction from Tree-rings and Its Relation to El Niño and the Southern Oscillation. The Holocene 1:95–101.

Dean, Jeffrey S., Robert C. Euler, George J. Gumerman, Fred Plog, Richard H. Hevley, and Thor N. V. Karlstrom

    1985   Human Behavior, Demography, and Paleoenvironment on the Colorado Plateau. American Antiquity 50:537–554.

Dean, Jeffrey S.

    1988   Dendrochronology and Environmental Reconstruction on the Colorado Plateau. In The Anasazi in a Changing Environment, edited by George J. Gumerman, pp. 119–167. Cambridge University Press.

Eddy, Frank W., Allen E. Kane, and Paul P. Nickens

    1984   Southwest Colorado Prehistoric Context. Colorado Historical Society, Office of Archaeology and Historic Preservation, Denver.

Ekren, E. B., and F. N. Houser
  1965   Geology and Petrology of the Ute Mountains Area, Colorado. Professional Paper 481. U. S. Geological Survey.
Euler, Robert C.
  1988   Demography and Cultural Dynamics on the Colorado Plateaus. In The Anasazi in a Changing Environment, edited by G. J. Gumerman, pp. 192–231. Cambridge University Press, Cambridge.
Euler, Robert C., George J. Gumerman, Thor N. V. Karlstrom, Jeffrey S. Dean, and Richard H. Hevly
  1979   The Colorado Plateaus: Cultural Dynamics and Paleoenvironment. Science 205:1089–1101.
Fetterman, Jerry, and Linda Honeycutt
  1987   The Mockingbird Mesa Survey, Southwestern Colorado. Cultural Resources Series 22. Bureau of Land Management, Denver.
Gellis, Allen, Richard Hereford, Stan A. Schumm, and B. R. Hayes
  1991   Channel Evolution and Hydrologic Variations in the Colorado River Basin: Factors Influencing Sediment and Salt Loads. Journal of Hydrology 124:317–344.
Gillespie, William B.
  1974   Culture Change at the Ute Canyon Site: A Study of the Pithouse–Kiva Transition in the Mesa Verde Region. Unpublished Master's Thesis, University of Colorado, Boulder.
Gleichman, Carol L., and Peter J. Gleichman
  1992   The Lower Sand Canyon Survey. In The Sand Canyon Archaeological Project, A Progress Report, edited by William D. Lipe, pp. 25-32. Occasional Paper 2. Crow Canyon Archaeological Center, Cortez, Colorado.
Gumerman, George J., (editor)
  1988   The Anasazi in a Changing Environment. School of American Research Advanced Seminar Series. Cambridge University Press, Cambridge.
Hack, John T.
  1942   The Changing Physical Environment of the Hopi Indians of Arizona. Papers of the Peabody Museum of American Archaeology and Ethnology Vol. 35, No.1. Harvard University, Cambridge.
Hall, Stephen A.
  1977   Late Quaternary Sedimentation and Paleoecologic History of Chaco Canyon, New Mexico. Bulletin No. 88. Geological Society of America.
Hereford, Richard, and R. H. Webb
  1992   Historic Variation of Warm-season Rainfall, Southern Colorado Plateau, Southwestern U. S.

A. Climatic Change 22:239–256.
Hevly, Richard H.
  1988   Prehistoric Vegetation and Paleoclimates on the Colorado Plateaus. In The Anasazi in a Changing Environment, edited by George J. Gumerman, pp. 92-118. School of American Research Advanced Seminar Series. Cambridge University Press, Cambridge.
Huff, Lyman C., and F. G. Lesure
  1965   Geology and Uranium Deposits of Montezuma Canyon Area, San Juan County, Utah. Bulletin 1190. U. S. Geological Survey.
Karlstrom, Thor N. V.
  1988   Alluvial Chronology and Hydrologic Change on Black Mesa and Nearby Regions. In The Anasazi in a Changing Environment, edited by George J. Gumerman, pp. 45–91. School of American Research, Advanced Seminar Series. Cambridge University Press, Cambridge.
Kidder, Alfred V.
  1927   Southwestern Archaeological Conference. Science 68:489–491.
Kuckelman, K. A., James Kleidon, Mark D. Varien, and Ricky R. Lightfoot
  1991   The 1990 Sand Canyon Project Site Testing Program: Preliminary Report of the Excavations at Saddlehorn (5MT262), Mad Dog Tower (5MT181), Castle Rock Pueblo (5MT1825), Lester's Site (5MT10246), Lookout House (5MT10459), and Cougar Cub Alcove (5MT1690). Report to Bureau of Land Management, San Juan Resource Area, Durango. Crow Canyon Archaeological Center, Cortez, Colorado.
Leopold, Luna B.
  1951   Rainfall Frequency: An Aspect of Climatic Variation. Transactions of the American Geophysical Union 32:347–357.
Lipe, William D.
  1992   Introduction. In The Sand Canyon Archaeological Project, A Progress Report, edited by William D. Lipe, pp. 1–10. Occasional Paper 2. Crow Canyon Archaeological Center, Cortez.
Lipe, William D., and Stephen Lekson
  1990   Southwestern Pueblo Cultures in Transition: Report of a Conference. Society for American Archaeology, Las Vegas.
Love, David W.
  1979   Quaternary Fluvial Geomorphic Adjustments in Chaco Canyon, New Mexico. In Adjustments of the Fluvial System, edited by D. D. Rhodes and G. P. Williams, pp. 277–308. Kendall/Hunt, Dubuque.

1983a Summary of the Late Cenozoic Geomorphic and Depositional History of Chaco Canyon. In Chaco Canyon Country, edited by S. G. Wells, David W. Love, and T. W. Gardner, pp. 187–194. American Geomorphological Field Group.

1983b Quaternary Facies in Chaco Canyon and Their Implications for Geomorphic-Sedimentologic Models. In Chaco Canyon Country, edited by S. G. Wells, David W. Love, and T. W. Gardner, pp. 195–206. American Geomorphological Field Group.

Orcutt, Janet D.
1991 Environmental Variability and Settlement Changes on the Pajarito Plateau, New Mexico. American Antiquity 56:315–332.

Oviatt, Charles G.
1985 Late Quaternary Geomorphic Changes Along the San Juan River and Its Tributaries Near Bluff, Utah. Special Studies 64. Utah Geological and Mineral Survey.

Packard, F. L.
1974 The Hydraulic Geometry of a Discontinuous Ephemeral Stream on a Bajada Near Tucson, Arizona. Unpublished Ph. D. dissertation, The University of Arizona, Tucson.

Petersen, Kenneth L.
1988 Climate and the Dolores River Anasazi: A Paleoenvironmental Reconstruction from a 10,000-year Pollen Record, La Plata Mountains, Southwestern Colorado. Anthropological Paper 113. University of Utah, Salt Lake City.

Plog, Fred, George J. Gumerman, Robert C. Euler, Jeffrey S. Dean, Richard H. Hevly, and Thor N. V. Karlstrom
1988 Anasazi Adaptive Strategies: The Model, Predictions, and Results. In The Anasazi in a Changing Environment, edited by G. J. Gumerman, pp. 230–276. School of American Research Advanced Seminar Series. Cambridge University Press, Cambridge.

Price, A B., W. D. Nettleton, G. A. Bowman, and V. L. Clay
1988 Selected Properties, Distribution, Source, and Age of Eolian Deposits and Soils of Southwest Colorado. Soil Science Society of America Journal 52:450–455.

Rohn, Arthur H.
1989 Northern San Juan Prehistory. In Dynamics of Southwest Prehistory, edited by Linda S. Cordell and George J. Gumerman, pp. 149–177. School of American Research Advanced Seminar Series. Smithsonian Institution Press, Washington, D.C.

Schlanger, Sarah H.
1988 Patterns of Population Movement and Long-term Population Growth in Southwestern Colorado. American Antiquity 53:773–793.

Schumm, Stanley A.
1973 Geomorphic Thresholds and the Complex Response of Drainage Systems. In Fluvial Geomorphology, edited by Marie Morisawa, pp. 299–310. State University of New York, Binghamton.

Schumm, Stanley A., M. D. Harvey, and C. C. Watson
1984 Incised Channels. Water Resources Publications, Littleton, Colorado.

Schumm, Stanley A., M. P. Mosely, and W. E. Weaver
1987 Experimental Fluvial Geomorphology. Wiley and Sons, New York.

Van West, Carla R., Michael A. Adler, and Edward K. Huber
1987 Archaeological Survey and Testing in the Vicinity of Sand Canyon Pueblo, Montezuma County, Colorado, 1986 Field Season. Report to Bureau of Land Management, San Juan Resource Area Office, Durango. Crow Canyon Archaeological Center, Cortez, Colorado.

Van West, Carla R., and William D. Lipe
1992 Modelling Prehistoric Climate and Agriculture in Southwestern Colorado. In The Sand Canyon Archaeological Project, A Progress Report, edited by W. D. Lipe, pp. 105–120. Occasional Paper 2. Crow Canyon Archaeological Center, Cortez, Colorado.

Vivian, R. Gwinn
1974 Conservation and Diversion: Water Control Systems in the Anasazi Southwest. In Irrigations Impact on Society, edited by Theodore E. Downing and McGuire Gibson, pp. 95–112. Anthropological Paper 25. The University of Arizona, Tucson.

Wanek, A. A.
1959 Geology and Fuel Resources of the Mesa Verde Area, Montezuma and La Plata Counties, Colorado. Bulletin 1072-M. U. S. Geological Survey, Boulder, Colorado.

Waters, Michael R.
1988 Holocene Alluvial Geology and Geoarchaeology of the San Xavier Reach of the Santa Cruz River, Arizona. Geological Society of America 100:479–491.

Webb, Robert H.
1985 Late Holocene Flooding on the Escalante River, South-central Utah. Unpublished Ph.D. dissertation, The University of Arizona, Tucson.

Weldon, R. J.

    1986 Late Cenozoic Geology of Cajon Pass: Implications for Tectonics and Sedimentation along the San Andreas Fault. Unpublished Ph.D. dissertation, California Institute of Technology.

Webb, Robert H., and Baker, V. R.

    1987 Changes in Hydrologic Conditions Related to Large Floods on the Escalante River, South-central Utah. In Regional Flood Frequency Analysis, edited by V. P. Singh, pp. 309–323. Reidel, New York.

Winter, Joseph C.

    1976 Hovenweep 1975. Archaeological Report 2. San Jose State University, San Jose.

    1977 Hovenweep, 1976. Archaeological Report 3. San Jose State University, San Jose.